ALSO BY JOHN FROHNMAYER

Leaving Town Alive: Confessions of an Arts Warrior

Out of Tune: Listening to the First Amendment

Socrates the Rower: How Rowing Informs Philosophy

Sunriver: A Legacy

SPIN! (musical comedy with Sila Shaman)

Carrying *the* Clubs

WHAT GOLF TEACHES US ABOUT ETHICS

John Frohnmayer

LUMINARE PRESS
WWW.LUMINAREPRESS.COM

Printed in the United States of America

Cover Design by Claire Flint Last
Cover photo background courtesy of Rogue Valley Country Club

Author photo by David Paul Bayles

"Ode to Bill," copyright © 1974 by John Ashbery; from *Self-Portrait in a
Convex Mirror* by John Ashbery. Used by permission of Viking Books, an imprint
of Penguin Publishing Group, a division of Penguin Random House LLC.
All rights reserved.

Luminare Press
442 Charnelton St.
Eugene, OR 97401
www.luminarepress.com

LCCN: 2019913571
ISBN: 978-1-64388-186-7

To the memory of
my brother and fellow caddie,
Dave Frohnmayer:
lived nobly; died too soon.

"I believe that everyone my age is an adult
and I am merely in disguise."

—MARGARET ATWOOD

"…Or, to take another example: last month
I vowed to write more. What is writing?
Well, in my case, it's getting down on paper
Not thoughts, exactly, but ideas, maybe:
Ideas about thoughts. Thoughts is too grand a word.
Ideas is better, though not precisely what I mean.
Someday I'll explain. Not today though."

—JOHN ASHBERY'S "ODE TO BILL,"
Self-Portrait in a Convex Mirror

TABLE OF CONTENTS

Part II
FAMILY REFLECTIONS

Part III
BEING CHURCHED

INTRODUCTION

The stories here are meant to be exemplary of moral principles that I learned as a caddie, as a golfer over much of my life (I have, for the time being, quit the game in disgust), and as an observer and participant in life.

Memories knock the rough edges off our experience so we can form and retell the narrative in a way that makes sense to us. This is why eyewitness testimony is so unreliable. We want to fill in the gaps—to make things make sense. At some point, we cannot tell the difference between what we have added and what we actually experienced. Oliver Sacks, who throughout his career did so much to help us understand how our brains work, writes of vivid memories of bombing in London during World War II when those memories were not his but those described by his brother in a letter.

Sacks sees this storing, forgetting, re-remembering, and reusing memories as the stuff of both creativity and mental health. Stories are the shelves on which we store memories, and while the stories I recount here of lessons from the golf course are true to the best of my memory, they are also meant to be exemplary, and so I may have tweaked them a bit. Call it artistic license.

Throughout this book, I use the terms morals and ethics interchangeably. My primary interest is where morals come from. How do we learn them? What are our sources? What do we take as authority and what as propaganda? In a reporter's role, how do we get to the who, what, where, why, and when of that we choose to believe and act on or desist from? How do we analyze our actions and failures? Where do shame, guilt, and regret come from?

The experiences from which I generalize are mine, since mine is the only life I have lived. We crank along in life skinning our knees, fudging our school work, telling our parents as little as we can get away with, and all of the sudden, we are adults operating with a playbook we didn't realize we had written. The little fibs and shortcuts that worked in the neighborhood work less well in the job and maybe not at all if the job is in the public eye.

From ages ten to fourteen, I caddied at the Rogue Valley Country Club in Medford, Oregon. A caddie spends a lot of time in the company of adults, is essentially invisible, and the adults are in an unguarded state. I listened and observed. I took the stories home to the dinner table. Most of the incidents were not indictable, and the statute of limitations is well past anyway.

My primary caveat is that there are likely more questions than answers here. That is the nature of philosophy and why the same questions have engaged humankind since humans began living together in groups. The search for the life well lived is one we all must undertake, and the answer that worked for the last generation may be inadequate today. To not ask the questions, to not seek the answers, is to ever remain a duffer in the game of life.

Since moral theory is based on reason, at least most of the time, and since golf is by definition an unreasonable game, how can one find guidance? Well, this could turn out to be merely a cautionary tale. All we can do is to keep asking why. Whether the answers we get are logical and satisfactory is what makes ethics a contact sport.

My last caveat is that I have not attempted to cloak my political leanings. I have contempt for both major political parties for their self-serving chicken-heartedness. I hope when you disagree with what I am writing, instead of tossing the book in a corner, you will go to the contact page on my website at www.johnfrohnmayer.com, and tell me, with a minimum of personal invective, where and why I am wrong. I would like to think that, by well-reasoned argument, I am persuadable.

PART I
Carrying the Clubs

CHAPTER 1

Mr. Smith

"The sting of conscience, like the gnawing of a
dog on a stone, is mere foolishness."

—Friedrich Nietzsche

L et's call him Mr. Smith because that was his name.
He wasn't a particularly good golfer. In fact, he was
terrible: whippy, inconsistent backswing, head movement at the top, lunge into the ball. The predictable result
was a grounder or for variety, as he did on number two tee,
a worm-burner that squirted sideways over the fence, out of
bounds, and into the tall weeds. A good caddie watches the
ball until it stops, but I had to jump out of the way to keep
from being hit, and the ball disappeared as soon as it crossed
the road, dislodging a long-eared jackrabbit that thumped
away in annoyance. I waded into the foxtails, but the parched
Southern Oregon hardpan meant it could have gone thirty
yards or stopped dead. There was a group waiting behind, so
he walked up about one hundred fifty yards, said he would
drop one there, and told me to come on. (Rules in dufferland
are a matter of convenience rather than necessity.)

We got done with our jobs early enough that my brother Dave and I went on a ball hunt. I loved looking for balls and found lots. Some were good enough to play with, some made it into my shag bag for practice with a classy, metallic-green stripe I painted around them, and some had been so abused as to be worthless. There, just off of number two tee, was Mr. Smith's ball, a shiny new Titleist. The next day when he walked into the pro shop, I gave it back to him.

He was surprised.

I knew I would feel bad about keeping it. I also knew his wife was a teacher. The word would get around about this unscheduled bit of honesty, and I knew that in a small town, reputation mattered a lot, even for kids. Did my less-than-pure motive besmirch the good deed? From a legal perspective, it was lost, and he probably had no further ownership rights to the ball, but I knew whose it had been. If I had kept it, would I have felt guilty? Probably. Where would that guilt have come from? If I had been a volunteer caddie, not getting paid, would the analysis change? Aristotle said that all paid jobs degrade, but that doesn't help much. I didn't go through any laborious analysis then. It was his ball, I was going to give it back, and I felt good about it when I did. No regrets.

Regrets are overrated anyway. Can't do anything about them, and they keep us looking backward rather than forward. We could have done better. We know that without having to dwell on our multiple shortcomings and omissions. In the words of the folk song, "I could have loved you better / didn't mean to be unkind / for you know that was / the last thing on my mind."

In his important book *On Becoming a Person,* psychologist Carl Rogers argues that we are healthiest when we are fully cognizant of all the experiences that have shaped us in our lives. That would include the ones about which we are sorry as well as our triumphs and achievements. That would include our guilt.

Most who have been educated in parochial schools don't have to scratch their heads wondering where guilt comes from. Others might opine that it is from Freud's superego. Maybe we are just inherently guilty—in a state of guilt instead of a state of grace. Otherwise, why would we immediately look at our speedometers when we hear a siren behind us? Inherent guilt, built in, hardwired, and microwavable, would fit nicely with Christianity's concept of original sin—if you believed that.

We want to confess. Trial lawyers, in preparing their witnesses and clients for cross-examination, preach "don't volunteer, don't speculate, listen to the question, answer that question and that question only, and stop." Most witnesses don't follow these instructions very well—they want to tell what they know. Lawyers on the witness stand themselves are the worst. I was called as a witness once, and I pontificated. I speculated. I was a disaster.

We are not one person but multiple persons acting differently in different roles, using different languages, working by different rules, and taking inconsistent positions. We feel guilty because we feel like a fraud. We fear we will be discovered. Embarrassed. Unclothed. We feel as if we are the only ones with this psychosis when all of us wear it to some degree.

The more prominent the person, the more likely that his or her different persons will serve different masters. This is one reason politicians seem so feckless. They are trying to serve their constituents, their party, their colleagues, and their donors, all of whom may have different interests. The more masters one must serve, the less individual freedom one has.

Back to Mr. Smith. I was sorry to part with the Titleist because it was brand new and my favorite ball. I would have to go out and find another one.

CHAPTER 2

On Becoming a Caddie

"How is nostalgia similar to an English lesson?
You find the present tense and the past perfect."

—Anonymous

Nothing about the pro shop at the Rogue Valley Country Club was grand. Glenn Jackson, known as Mr. Oregon because of his work on the Transportation Commission that built the interstate, his king-making in politics, and his general presence in most everything that mattered, owned the course and subsidized it so that players of modest income could afford the dues. His largess did not extend to the pro shop, which was low ceilinged and plain with a small fireplace on the left, a counter straight ahead, a cubby with benches for caddies on the right, and lockers, club storage, a shoeshine area, and a candy counter. Al Williams was the pro with Eddie Oldfield, and later Vince Alexa, as assistants.

Lots of waiting around. Dad would drop Dave and me off on his way to the office around 8 a.m. Bus service was available but infrequent, and caddies such as Eugene McFadden, Tom "Heavy" Harper, Phil Mongrain, and others arrived when the bus saw fit. Sometimes Eddie Oldfield entertained us by balancing three golf balls on top of each other. Try it—two is easy, three requires a steadiness of touch I could accomplish neither then nor now. The main source of entertainment was playing blackjack for golf tees, and Dave and I were wily cardsharps as was witnessed by cigar boxes full of short, medium, and long tees. He was "Mad Dog," and I was "Bull." All of us took turns being dealer, and cheating was not unknown. Trust but verify as Ronald Reagan would later say—or maybe it was Kennedy. Not sure if either of them hung around with caddies much.

Al Williams led the caddie lessons, usually on Mondays when the course was closed. Stay ahead, stay quiet, and pay attention. A caddie who picks up a bag and slings the clubheads back of his shoulder is a seventy-five-cents-per-round rookie. Don't step in any player's line when taking the pin. Face the ball that is away so the players don't have to ask. Give advice, like club selection, only when asked, but you should be able to club your player by the second hole. Watch every shot until it stops, not just the shot of your player. Keep the score card neatly, and ask if you are uncertain what a player shot on the last hole (or how many he was willing to admit). Don't rattle the clubs when a player is addressing the ball. Don't fart.

Phil Mongrain was the head caddie. I don't know if that was a title bestowed by management or just one he had because he was older, more experienced, or pretty smart and pretty mouthy. He and Eddie Oldfield got into it one day over something incidental, and Eddie said, "You're fired" with an operatic gesture toward the door. First time I had ever witnessed a firing, and while not an old-time hanging, it was impressive. The next day, Mongrain reappeared, came into the pro shop, and stood in front of the fire with a small grin. We waited. Eddie didn't. "You come back to clean out your locker?" Headshake. "Phil." Operatic gesture toward the door. That was it. He did eventually return to caddying, but his mantle was tarnished, and the rest of us gave Eddie a wide berth.

Eddie was a talented golfer albeit a bit wild. On number thirteen (old, old course), a par 5 with out of bounds along the right side, Eddie hit a big drive, a big and errant second that bounced off an oak tree out of bounds and went onto the green and into the hole. An albatross or double eagle. He also had some stories about stuff with girls that I was too young to fully appreciate.

To recap, the ten commandments of caddying are:

1. Stay ahead.

2. Stay quiet.

3. Pay attention.

4. Don't step in a player's line when taking the pin.

5. Face the ball that is away so they don't have to ask.

6. Give advice only when asked and then be right.

7. Watch every shot until it stops.

8. Keep the score card accurately (except when told not to).

9. Don't rattle the clubs when the player is hitting

10. Don't fart.

We'll deal with the other ten commandments later.

CHAPTER 3

Rules of Golf

"Golf is so popular simply because it is the best
game in the world at which to be bad."

—A. A. MILNE,
author of *Winnie the Pooh*

The rules of golf have been piling up since 1744 when
the Gentlemen Golfers of Leith, Scotland, got serious about the game. This didn't stop members from
ripping holes in their pockets so they could "find" balls lost
in the rough, and like laws everywhere, some rules were made
to be broken. Golf has always patted itself on the back as the
only sport in which players call penalties on themselves, and
there are no referees with whistles watching over play. Anyone
involved in playground pickup basketball knows how effective
calling fouls on one's self is.

Some rules such as "play it as it lies" sound like "dance
with the one that brung ya" or "play the hand you're dealt" and
strike me as generally bad advice from a moral standpoint. The
course setup can be diabolical. I have seen tee markers set so
that if you hit a straight ball from between them, you would

be in the woods. This is the kind of societal misdirection that the existentialist philosopher Soren Kierkegaard railed against: Society's advice is not to be trusted. The term tee box, incidentally, comes from the early Scottish practice of having a box with sand in it that the players used to make a small mound under their ball before hitting.

I have always loved the rules about "casual water." As opposed to what? Serious water? Formal water?

In a frontal assault on the criticism that the game is stogy, the Professional Golfers Association (PGA) cranked out thirty-seven new rules for 2019, and with what I am sure is breathless anticipation on your part, here are some of them.

When relief from a position where the ball has stopped is allowed, the ball must be dropped straight down from knee height (used to be shoulder) when the knee is straight. Whose knee? The player's knee, and it can't hit the player on the way down, but if it rolls against his shoe or equipment, it is in play.

If a dropped ball rolls out of a relief area twice, it can be placed where the second drop hit. If it rolls from there, it may be placed where it will stay but no nearer the hole.

A relief area is equal to the length of the longest club carried in the player's bag but not the putter. A relief area, by the way, is not a restroom under the rules.

If the ball accidentally hits you after, say, being deflected off a bank, or hits your equipment, no penalty. Play it where it lies. It used to be a two-stroke penalty if you bounced one off your golf cart.

A double hit is now a single stroke. A double hit is like a soft wedge shot where the follow-through hits the ball in the air.

There is no penalty for carrying a nonconforming club,

only for using it, so that bazooka in my bag…well, just you don't worry about it.

If an "outside influence," say, a bear playing on the green, moves your ball, it will be replaced but never dropped, *even if the spot is not known.* Whoa, we will need a judge to deal with this one.

You can now remove stones, dead deer, and animal scat from bunkers without penalty.

A water hazard is now a penalty area.

Damage to the green may now be repaired (spike marks, divots, etc.) but must be done "promptly" and does not include "natural wear of the hole." Here come da judge.

No one can help a player align a shot, but the caddie may stand behind his player aligning a putt so long as the player backs away and starts again without the caddie directly behind him. *Come on, man!*

These rules would make a Pharisee blush. Here are a few rules I would like to see, and some of these are stolen from or inspired by Henry Beard's book *The Official Exceptions to the Rules of Golf.*

If on the first tee, the drive of a brand-new ball goes into the water, the player may hit again with no penalty. This reminds me of original sin. There is the pristine ball, sleeping with the fishes like Luca Brasi, and it is faultless.

A ball hit in the middle of the fairway and not found has clearly been filched by supernatural forces through no fault of the golfer. Drop one where it should have been.

On golf courses with multiple tees you may, without penalty, play a forward set on any hole: a) if you feel like it, b) that is sufficiently intimidating from your set, or c) if no one is looking.

A whiff doesn't count if: a) you immediately yell "jeofails," an old English common law remedy for a mistake, b) your playing partners are laughing inappropriately, or c) you are persuaded you really didn't try to hit the thing.

A ball coming to rest in a yard adjacent to the fairway may be retrieved and dropped without penalty if: a) no large dog is present, b) the ball is new, or c) the damage to the property is slight, i.e., below felony level.

You may take action up to and including minor bodily harm to any annoying playing partner who: a) uses his fucking cell phone, b) narrates every shot, c) reputts every miss while the group behind waits.

Any shot where the distance of the divot exceeds that of the ball may be taken over without penalty. Feel free to wipe the mud off your face first.

After I hit, if you ask what club I used, it is a two-stroke penalty only if I tell you the truth.

If you are looking for moral lessons here, there are few to none, but it does bring up a distinction worth mention: The law and ethics are different. The law says you must or you can't, and if you disobey, you will be punished—jailed or fined. Ethics say you should or shouldn't, and if you choose wrongly, your punishment is from your own head (guilt), from society's shit list (shame), or in the great hereafter (heaven or hell).

CHAPTER 4

Social Roles and Service

"When all is said and done, style is function
and function is style."

—BEN HOGAN

Rules are rules, but style and substance were constantly on display. The flashy Clayton Lewis, whom all the others called "Old Dad," the sweet-swinging duffer Bob Lockwood, and the serene and unbeatable Eddie Simmons, who after long absence would show up, hit a bag of balls, and win the Southern Oregon Tournament—these were some of the adults in my life as a caddie. Tension was a word unknown to me then; life was to be lived, and each day brought something new and interesting. I did appreciate that these men, and indeed some women, represented life choices and lifestyles, but I was just cruising along—a kid with his eyes open to watch, listen, and absorb.

Carol Jo Kabler's fat father drove a Cadillac, but you could tell by looking at him that he was not a Cadillac guy. No class, and anyway, his was a '55, and it was 1957, and no self-respecting Cadillac guy drove one that was two years old.

John Frohnmayer

No sir. The car defined the man, not vice versa.

I was up practicing on old number eleven when Carol Jo came striding up in her Bermuda shorts, cigarette pack in hand, and sat down on the grass next to my practice balls as if we had known each other for years. She became famous by emerging from the nowhere town of Sutherlin to be the best female golfer Southern Oregon had seen. Here she was, smoking (Mother didn't like her for that reason alone), commenting occasionally on one of my shots, and passing the time in a most pleasant way. I liked her. After she turned pro and changed to her married name, I looked for results in the paper occasionally, but she faded into the vapor of my life as a momentary image that proved a chance meeting could change my mind about someone.

Cars were to the 1950s what clothes were to the Victorians. A Ford or a Chevy, even a new one, was either the second car of a prosperous, middle-class person or the first car of a worker. A Pontiac was classier, racier for a young professional, particularly the ones with the parallel chrome strips running up the back. Oldsmobiles, except for the ones with the spinner hubcaps, and Buicks were middle-class family cars. A Cadillac said you had made the big time, or at least you aspired, while a Lincoln or even a Chrysler said you had made it but were content to preen quietly. Convertibles were the cat's ass.

When Dr. Bayuck drove up in his blue-and-white Buick Roadmaster with the two chrome handles on the trunk, I rushed out to help him unload his clubs and gear (he was from Northern California and drove up with his pals to play the best course around). He paid $3.50 a round, which was top of the caddie pay scale. When Felix Secott arrived in a Mercedes 180 diesel, none of us knew what to make of it. Noisy, smelly, and boxy. Only much later would I come to treasure that vertical Mercedes grill, the red leather, and the off-white paint. The first Corvette—well, what can you say—was beyond wonderful.

Caddying was recreational for me. Yes, I was working and getting paid for it, but how hard is it to walk around a golf course? The best part was seeing the adults up close with their usual societal defenses stowed away. Sometimes I was in the role of confessor: Ray Mencke told me it was easier to put the flask they were passing around to his lips and not drink than to refuse it on a cold winter Saturday morning (I didn't care or judge). Sometimes I was a confidant as when old Dr. Fox, who took down the big-hitting Wayne Sabin, half his age, told me, "Sometimes I have my wedge working like a scalpel." A healer and an assassin.

Hogan's statement about style and function at the head of this chapter puts him squarely in the philosophical camp of the American pragmatist William James. The golf swing that works is the right one; the ethical rule that works is the right one. When it stops working, get a new one that does. Simple and very, very hard.

The role of a caddie was unambiguous: you were there to serve, do what you were told, carry the clubs, take the pins, and otherwise be invisible. From that role came certain moral imperatives such as being polite and not swinging your master's clubs or rummaging through his bag for stuff to steal, but otherwise there weren't many moving parts—not a lot of thorny moral issues. At the same time, I never remember the role of a caddie as being anything other than noble. Not noble in some royalty sense but being worthy, honest, and worthwhile. Likewise, I never thought of doing anything other than the best job I could do.

I recognized, without thinking much about it, that I was working for the pay as opposed to lending my puny effort to some transcendental social cause, but the effort was the same whether I was on the bag of one of the old boys for a buck a nine or one of the doctors for a buck fifty. The cause I was working for was my education. The deal with Dad was that he would match all the money we put in our savings accounts, and it would go toward our college education. I had a little bank book in which the teller would write my deposits in ink, and I took great pleasure in seeing it grow.

Did I define myself by my job, and did my job define me? Later in life, did I define myself as a lawyer? Hold those thoughts. My Dad did define himself as a lawyer. He loved the law and loved the small-town role of being the go-to guy for issues that needed the attention of a smart, canny craftsman of words and strategies. That's who he was to the world outside the family. To the family, he was lovingly distant except to Mother, whom he adored. He expected us to produce, be the best we could be, and reflect well on the family. "Remember who you are and what you represent."

As a kid, did I define myself as a caddie? No, I was just a kid. Even as a lawyer in my working-for-pay days, I don't think I defined myself as a lawyer. I would be more comfortable describing myself as an athlete, a singer, a husband and father, and an arts lover. I was pleased to acknowledge that I did the law for a living because I consider it a worthy profession, one of service, but it didn't seem that that was who I was. I often wondered if, as a geezer looking backward, I would ponder if I had chosen the wrong path for my life. Should

I have been a singer/actor in musical comedy, a diplomat or, shudder, a writer?

Even those questions were the wrong questions. I always thought of myself not as a job but as a being in the world, both as a citizen actor and an observer. Still do. A caddie is a servant, and that role never bothered me in the least.

The pressing question today is how we as a society will deal with a world in which artificial intelligence and robotics have eliminated most of what we now call work and there aren't enough jobs to go around. No longer hypothetical, this time is upon us. Will we take the opportunity to redefine work as service to others, as a society where everyone is entitled to a guaranteed standard of living including food, housing, and individual dignity? Will craftspersons be honored for the meticulous execution of exquisite objects, prized for their beauty alone? Will we substitute communal activities such community gardens, singing together, reading, and amateur sports for what we now call work? Will the question change from "what do you do" to "what do you value"? This is hardly a new description of the good life. The first century BCE Roman poet Ovid said, "Nothing is more useful to man than those arts which have no utility."

Such a society would provide the opportunity for what Aristotle defined as real friendships. He saw three kinds: mutual attraction, convenience (what each can do for the other in business or other daily activities), and substantive friendships that could flourish in a society of abundant leisure. These would be the friendship of souls who are virtuous, meaning that each has found and practiced the golden mean of moderation in all things. Freed of the imperative to make a living, people could study, think, and practice the creation of a life.

If money were not the measure of value, the society could be more virtuous. In the Christian tradition, love of money is the root of all evil (1 Timothy 6:10). Perhaps a new piety could spring up in which helping and serving were the valued currency. Families would have more time and leisure for child-rearing. Preserving the environment would be every nation's obsession. Self-education would be a lifelong passion with ample time and support to make it rewarding. Sounds utopian, but change is upon us, and if we are moral, it is our duty to try to direct it, not just let it happen.

While I was growing up in the '50s, we turned our morals over to corporations, and we couldn't have made a more Faustian bargain. "What is good for General Motors is good for America" may be an inaccurate quote of what GM's president said, but the sense that corporations were necessary, good, and could be trusted and admired was universal. The problem is that the very nature of the corporate entity is immoral: Its purpose is to maximize profit and minimize responsibility. It has unlimited life and no obligation to be a good citizen. Corporations don't go to church, fight in wars or, in many cases, even pay taxes. Those who run them seldom go to jail for corporate misdeeds such as polluting the earth, killing people, and selling adulterated products. The phrase "shareholders' rights" is an oxymoron. Corporate advertising urges us to buy that which we don't need, which can harm us (alcohol and cigarettes, for example), or which is unlikely to help us ("Ask your doctor if _____ is right for you").

Since a corporation is a fictitious legal construct, and since those who act on behalf of the corporation, including those who invest in it, are normally not liable for its actions or debts, any morality that might have been attached is at least one step removed from another human. It is easier to lie to or on behalf of a fictitious entity than it is face to face with another person. The pressures to return profits to shareholders or to justify the enormous salaries of officers encourage shortcuts in quality, ill treatment of workers (such as moving manufacturing offshore), and crappy products. In short, a corporation is a lousy moral model.

I'm not saying an economic system based on capital is inherently evil, just that it is an economic system, not a moral one. For a moral system, we need to consider social capital that includes building trust in a society, the recognition that people's skills constitute value, granting without qualification individual dignity to every person, and appreciating skill in interpersonal relations as a critical element of a functioning society.

At a minimum, this means telling the truth as we see it, avoiding gratuitous cruelty, and keeping our tribal instincts in check. It includes empathy, and empathy requires volunteers—those who help others without expectation of reward. In many ways this was the society Alexis de Tocqueville saw in the 1830s and about which he wrote in *Democracy in America*. That was a society of voluntary associations. What we have now is a society that asks first "what's in it for me?"

CHAPTER 5

Practicing Heroes

"Don't groove your waggle."

—BEN HOGAN

S hagging may mean something quite different across the pond in randy old England, but to us caddies, it meant dumping a canvas bag of golf balls at the feet of your master on the practice range, trudging down however far he said with bag in hand, and picking up the balls as he hit them. Hit them right at you. You were the target.

Good eyesight was obviously a benefit. Paying attention too. Usually he (almost always a *he*) started out with short irons: wedge, 9, and 8. The advantage was that you were closer and the shots generally higher and easier to follow in the air. Downside was if he skulled one, it was a laser coming right at you. As he worked back into the longer clubs, particularly the woods, things got more aerobic. For a big hook, he would hold out his left arm, and you would start running in that direction, trying to locate the ball in the air. Sometimes you found it, sometime not. Opposite with the slice, but if your master was a slicer,

God help you, because he was probably a duffer, and the ball could go anywhere.

The practice range was an open field between number ten and number eighteen fairways (old course). At about two hundred yards, the oak woods started, which meant that you were dodging trees and trying to find out where the ball deflected. In retrospect, the solution to shagging generally would have been to return with a half-full bag and a big shrug, but I was far too conscientious for such a response. Joe Burns, a neighbor two years my senior, got hit right below the eye with a ball, and his face swelled up flat with his nose. I don't remember any consequence; shagging continued unabated.

The golf ball in the face example injects the possibility of luck into the moral equation. Joe wasn't hit by accident. He was the target. The guy who hit him probably felt bad, but he couldn't escape the possibility that his caddie would be hit. What if the ball had killed him? Lifelong guilt for the hitter, perhaps prosecution by a conscientious district attorney but probably not. A civil action for wrongful death? Unlikely in those days. The luck part is that all of the facts are the same except in one case it was an injury and in another, death. Luck plays a major role in where you are born, who your parents are, and the genes you end up with that determine your brains, health, and physical abilities. Life isn't fair. That isn't a moral concept, simply the truth. The morality part is that we have to deal with it.

Dave and I had our own shag bags, his balls painted with a metallic-blue stripe and mine, metallic-green. The balls were the booty from our ball hunts and were greatly prized. The difference was that we would hit them, pick up the bag, and go down and retrieve them ourselves, often dodging the missiles from others who weren't about to interrupt their slugging.

I never liked to practice much, which explains why my golf game never progressed beyond my natural talent. When I did practice, I hit balls one after another—wham, wham, wham. I wasn't aiming, wasn't trying to hit a fade or a draw. I was flailing away and learning nothing. Professional golfers, instead of going to the showers or the bar like most athletes, go to the practice range when they finish their rounds. That is the time when they can fix what didn't go well or solidify what did.

One young lady named Alicia was a good hitter, and she practiced all the time. Never played. On the rare occasion when she ventured on the course, she rocketed an approach twenty yards over the green and was perplexed.

The heroes of the day were Ben Hogan and Sam Snead. Hogan was taciturn, intense, brooding. He was injured in an auto accident where he threw himself in front of his wife to protect her before the bus crushed their car—at least that is the way the movie portrayed it. He was untouchable, he of the "Hogan fade," the perfect grip, the steely nerves. He said, "I play with friends, but we don't play friendly games." So untouchable was he that he bore no nickname (we didn't buy the "Bantam Ben" stuff; to us he was a giant). He had a gallows sense of humor. Asked for advice by a young hopeful, he said, "Watch out for buses." He figured out that putts break toward the west, and teaching great Harvey Penick agrees. Really?

Snead, on the other hand, was "Slammin' Sammy" with his straw fedora and perfect rhythm. He and Hogan would duke it out for titles, for endorsements, for adulation among the ordinary mortals whose occasional good shot kept them coming back to the course each week and invaded their desk dreams. Golfer Peter Thompson said of Snead, "Like the classic plays and symphonies, Sam Snead doesn't belong to just one generation. His mark will be left on golf for an eternity." Snead, in responding to ribbing from baseball great Ted Williams, said that when golfers hit a foul ball, they have to find it and play it. Snead won eighty-one tournaments and, from a standing start, could jump and kick the ceiling.

Jackie Burke had his name on some clubs I had, and one day Julius Boros, another touring pro, showed up at the club to play a round. Big guy. Slow, controlled swing. Good putter. I learned by watching what he did, how he walked, what he said to his caddie. He was a winner but not a showboat. He was willing to play in the rain without an umbrella. He was a mortal, not a god—the nearest thing to a celebrity I had seen. The story goes that he hired a local caddie (not at our club) and told the kid, who was looking dumbly at a divot, to pick it up. On the second nine, the kid got farther and farther behind, and Boros asked if he was sick. The kid said no, but what do you want me to do with these? The whole side pocket of Boros' bag was full of divots.

A few days after Boros' exhibition, I drew a job caddying for a pair of men from Canada. They were in Medford for an unknown reason and wanted to play on a rainy afternoon. Their banter was light. "You didn't acknowledge those ladies when they let us play through." "I tipped my hat; what did you want me to do, run up and kiss 'em?" They were surprised that I replaced all of their divots. "In Canada, we let them lie around." I think they were messing with me. When we were done, they gave me some funny-looking bills—Canadian money. I stared at it. The numbers were right, but what the hell was I supposed to do with it? They laughed and gave me real dollars. "Keep the loonies," they said. I had no idea what they were talking about.

Heroes arrived in my life in much more modest circumstance. A player who bought you a soda (a Big Orange) was a fine fellow. Justin Smith, he of the returned Titleist, hired Tom Harper to caddie. I was in the group on the bag of another player. Tom allowed as how he "didn't wipe so good"—it was sort of a public announcement—and was getting butt cheek burn. Justin whipped out his trusty pocketknife and whittled a cheek spreader from a dead branch. Many of the players had been in World War II, and that can-do spirit was very much alive. I marveled at Tom McCloud, who announced Medford football games on the radio and made it around the course on his wooden leg. He never complained although his stump was sometimes bloody at the end.

CHAPTER 6

A Funny Game

"He who laughs, lasts."
—MIKE NICHOLS, film director

A CBS sports announcer for the Masters Tournament, acknowledging the solemn tradition of the event, said, "Nothing funny ever happens at Augusta. Dogs don't bark, and babies don't cry. They wouldn't dare." Tradition is a big deal in golf. Sometimes it is honoring the best about the game. Sometimes it is worshipping the ashes of what is long gone. A green jacketed official told a weary spectator that he could not doze with his back against a tree; not at Augusta.

Golf is play, and isn't play supposed to be fun? Not at the level the pros play it. For them, it is the most prolonged test of the most slavish concentration required of any sport. Golf great Walter Hagen was heard to say in the 1920s, "Give me a man with big hands and big feet and no brains, and I will make a golfer out of him." No more. Big hands and feet may help, but the pros acknowledge that careful thinking and singular concentration is the combination that wins tournaments.

John Frohnmayer

Humor is a form of play, and play is a necessary part of existence. Animals play as infants to learn the skills to hunt, escape, and survive. They know inherently the soft bite and sheathed claws so they will not injure or kill their playmate. As night follows day, philosophers study play to try to make sense of it. The father of modern play theory, the Dutch philosopher John Huizinga, published the book *Homo Ludens* in 1938. (Ludens is the Latin root of ludicrous, and you, my friend, are a homo.) Not surprisingly, he concluded that human play is different from that of other animals. That should be no surprise since we are such colossally bad sports, but that was not one of his four distinctions. First, play is free from normal societal constraints (like in boxing, where the idea is to hit the opponent). Second, it makes up its own rules. Third, it is a world of its own and, in that sense, is an escape from the real world. Fourth, play is its own reward; most people do it for the pure pleasure of the activity rather than for money. Does that analysis make your life fuller, richer? Not so much, I think.

Golf was so formative to me as a young caddie because it was a prolonged opportunity to observe adults. They would swear, cheat, drink, talk about their indiscretions, and otherwise display a self their jobs and homelife would not allow. Little did they know that I was absorbing all of this for the evening's dinner table hilarity.

Humiliation is the stock and trade of both the game of golf and of humor. I heard one guy say after he forgot his ball in the ball washer, "I don't mind losin' 'em on the course, but when I lose 'em in the ball washer, it's time to quit." Served him right, because it was my job to wash the ball.

Golf opens the floodgates of lost opportunities. It is the street of broken dreams; it strips the soul naked; it exposes our foibles. Here is a golf joke: Husband comes home, and wife asks how his day went. He says terrible, Henry died on the third hole. That's awful, says she. He says, yeah, all the rest of the way 'round, it was hit the ball, drag Henry, hit the ball, drag Henry.

Because the golfer is essentially trapped in an abusive relationship with an unforgiving, mean-spirited course, a round can dull the senses. I was coming off the Stanford course bemoaning lost opportunities when in the parking lot, as if in a vision, I saw a girl named Ashleigh, whom I liked very much but hadn't the courage to ask out again. She tossed her clubs in the trunk of what was clearly her parents' car, slammed the lid down, and turned to me with a big smile. I muttered some sort of desultory greeting and trudged on. Only too late did it dawn on me that she was waiting for me, and I was the world's greatest doofus.

Here is some stuff you should know to improve your game, so I will quote it at length:

> *With sleep deprivation, the connectivity of the amygdala to the ventromedial prefrontal cortex is weakened. The amygdala initiates a fear response but cannot act without the approval of the prefrontal cortex. Connectivity between the insula and the amygdala are increased magnifying the fear response. As basic as it sounds, getting a minimum of seven to eight hours of uninterrupted sleep is crucial—for much more than we realize. Just getting back those few extra hours each week can be the difference that pushes us to go the extra mile...rather than to play it safe and keep our deepest fears at bay.*[1]

---

1   James Sullivan, *Always At the Back of Our Minds: Exploring the Science of Anxiety. Brainworldmagazine.com. January 2019.*

This must have been what happened to me with Ashleigh. I was in college, and getting seven to eight uninterrupted hours of sleep was unheard of. Either that or a grass clod had wedged open the sensory gate of my thalamus.

Apropos of trunk slamming, if, as a pro, you do it on Friday afternoon, it means that you didn't make the cut, and you are on your way to the next event or to some other kind of work.

CHAPTER 7

Fear, Success, and Goal Setting

"Horse sense is what keeps horses
from betting on people."

—W. C. Fields

I t was either Charlie Brown from Fort Jones or Charlie Jones from Fort Brown. The former, I think. His friends were Ken Phelps, a big guy named Fireworker, and one or two more. They drove up from Northern California to play, and play they did: $100 per hole. As a caddie, I was agog. One hundred dollars was a lot of money in the mid '50s, and sometimes the bet would be a hundred if he got a piece of the hole on a putt. I never saw the money change hands. Maybe it was all a sham, but it seemed real, and when Ken Phelps was lining up a put and said, "don't rattle the clubs, caddie," I was a pillar of salt.

One time, Fireworker was messing around, using the head of his driver as a pretend microphone, and Charlie Brown (or Jones) was in the lower trap on the steeply uphill eleventh hole.

Brown (Jones) flubbed the shot, and Fireworker said, "Done like a pro. Say a word into the mic," to which Brown /Jones said, "Shit." I took that amusement home to the dinner table.

The California guys were playing for big bucks, but the real pressure was for the Southern Oregon tourney title, and year after year, Eddie Simmons seemed to be in contention. His clubs were old, his putter a simple blade, and his swing tight and compact. On number fifteen, he was in the trees to the left of the par 3 green. He looked up and topped his shot cold, and it rolled through the trees, through the grass trap up onto the green, and into the hole. That was Eddie Simmons. Nobody can teach that stuff.

I caddied a lot for Sue DeVoe, who usually made it to the women's final. I don't remember her winning. I do remember over clubbing her on number sixteen and watching her superb strike airmailing the green. She was a good sport about it; I was mortified. My sister, Mira, was playing one year. She had a long, fluid swing and great timing but not great nerves. Freddie Haupert was following along and saying out of earshot of her opponent. "Come on, swivel hips, shank it into the trap." Such was our sportsmanship. Mira won. She was a fine athlete.

One lesson that golf teaches, at least it is there to be learned if you want, is to set your own rules, your own standards for success. Singer Willie Nelson is an unlikely looking golf fanatic: gray beard, ponytail, dumpster clothes. He built his own course at his home in Austin, Texas. He has his own rules, his own playing partners, his own setup. He says, "One hole is a par 23, and yesterday I almost birdied the sucker."

I've been told one should prepare for a round of golf like a trial lawyer does for a trial. As a lifelong trial lawyer, if that were true, I would never play. If more than 4 percent of what happens in a trial is a surprise, you are going to lose. That means meticulous preparation, exhaustive discovery, endless witness preparation, thoroughly researched briefs, jury consultants, focus groups, and dozens of other worries. You know opposing counsel is doing the same, and although the combat in the courtroom once the trial starts is exhilarating, the preparation is nothing but anxiety. Why would I do that to play a round of golf?

Most don't. That is why certain situations in golf are scary. We are unprepared for them. Here are the five scariest: a shot over water, particularly tee to green; a short finesse chip over a bunker to the green; the shot off the first tee, particularly if a gallery is watching; your first long putt; and a recovery shot from the woods.

Were we to do the trial lawyer preparation, we would practice thusly: on water shots, hit down on the ball so it will go up, aim for a small spot on the green so your focus will not be on the water, take a club more than you need so you will swing easy, do the Buddhist-yoga-mind-flushing thing, and use an old ball (kidding). Playing and practicing are two different things. You can't practice while playing. It's too late; the band is rocking, and the dance has begun.

For the short chip over a bunker, hit enough wedge shots that you have confidence in the club, your rhythm, and your distance judgment. Keep your damn head down. Know that the best you can do may leave you with a twenty-foot putt. Similar advice for the first tee, i.e., don't psyche yourself out. Trust your swing, clear your mind, don't try to kill it, don't hit your weapon of mass destruction, nine-degree driver if you can't control it. If you didn't spend the little time you left for warm-up on the putting green, you will 3 putt the first long one. Serves you right, and who said this game was supposed to be fun? Best advice for the woods, other than don't get in there in the first place, is that the quickest way out is the best way out. That last phrase is also a criminal defense lawyer's mantra.

Here are the four most feared moral situations for comparison. First is betraying a spouse, second, confronting racist friends, third, saying "I'm sorry," and fourth, correcting a long-standing wrong. There are plenty of comparisons between the lack of rehearsal for a well-played golf game and the bumbling, mealy mouthed, thoughtless, dork-headed mess we make of our lives and relationships by moral fumbling. Plato taught that to be moral beings, we should practice moral behavior, we should emulate the actions of a moral leader, we should seek neither excess nor deprivation. Moderation in moral behavior could mean preserving the dignity of all involved rather than winning a point at a Pyrrhic cost. It could mean not escalating into ad hominem attacks like "you are just like your mother" to which the rejoinder is likely to be "if you could see over your beer gut, you would know how pathetic your wanger is." Nothing good can come from this.

Given how badly we do at most of life, it is a testament to the resiliency of the human spirit that we keep coming back for more. It is also the reason religion is a staple of many people's lives. In golf, a single good shot can inspire dreams of greatness and keep a sucker coming back for more. Pro golfer Jeff Sluman says, "I hate this game, and I can't wait till tomorrow to play again."

The philosopher of golf might ask why the whole hole is called a hole. The goal for the whole hole is to get the ball in the hole. I get that, but every hole has a tee box, a fairway, sometimes trees and water, lots of grass, and a green, and somewhere on that green is a hole. All of those are collectively a hole. Strange. That hole (and here I am meaning the round thing with a 4½-inch space between its edges) can be—no, is—diabolical. It can swallow a ball, but it also can spit one out or ride it around the rim to spin out or disappear. It can wink at the ball as it goes by, laugh at the ball that hangs on the edge, never to drop. It can perform the thump and jump where a ball coming in like a carrier landing hits the back of the hole, leaps into the air, and falls in. The ball can skip over the void of the hole as if it weren't there and cruise onto the far side of the green. Nobody tells a hole what to do; it has a mind of its own. Golf great Greg Norman missed a one-foot putt at the British Open.

Let's ditch the sexual analogies of the pin and the hole and slide right into Saint Augustine's theory of alienation. Actually, it was Aristotle, but cut me some slack. God created all things, and all things he created are good. Therefore, he couldn't have created evil. Evil is like a hole in a shirt. The hole isn't matter; it isn't a thing, but it is something to be dealt with, and it is in dealing with issues of the void, like the golf hole, that humankind has become alienated. Okay, neither Aristotle nor Augustine played golf, nor did they foresee that multiple millennia later the game would become all the rage, but doesn't this sound right? This joyless plod down the emerald-green fairways of indifference has thrust humankind into a bad mood for the last five hundred years, and that obnoxious hole is to blame.

There. Now that we have had that theological lesson, let's get down to the business of how to deal with that little bastard. Luck is good. You played it to break right and stubbed it horribly, and it broke hard left and went in. High fives all around. You know in your heart of hearts that this is no way to live life. Luck is a Janus-faced harpy. Talking to the ball doesn't work either. No ball ever made speaks your language.

First thing is to read the green. You look, squatting down behind the ball, and it looks like six inches outside the right edge. You look at it from behind the hole and it looks "slightly straight." You look at the green and try to decide, if you were water, where you would go. You get back behind the ball and hold up your putter shaft like a plumb line. This tells you squat. You remember Hogan said putts break to the west. Which way is west? Your playing partners are grousing at you to hit the damn thing, so that is what you do. Get up there and hit it.

Here are some semi-theological tips. Visualize the hole, and bring it back to you. Becalm yourself. Think of the four Buddhist steps of stopping, calming, resting, and healing, and then play the shot from the stillness. Once you are over the ball, let the swing happen. This is the Nike "Just Do It" moment where the practice you have done to train your muscles should come into play. Listen for the putt to drop into the hole (in other words, keep your head down). Finally, on long putts, be content with a 2 putt. Not every swing is a challenge for greatness. Stay in the moment. Think of your dog—she is an expert at this.

CHAPTER 8

Being Content with the Not So Perfect

"What is the most important shot in golf?
The next one."

—BEN HOGAN

Drinking alcohol was part of being an adult in the '50s. Smoking too. My parents drank a cocktail before dinner, but neither smoked. Their friends did both. One time, Bill and Sue Barker had a breakfast party, and Bill had made five-gallon plastic gas cans of martinis, one of vodka and one of gin. One guest became inspired to stand on her head while dressed in a skirt. That is about as close to sex education as I got. The only lesson from Mother (Dad was silent) was, "Don't do it."

At the country club, the bar was visible to us kids, because it adjoined the dining room. One female patron was standing at the bar and keeled over backwards, her head hitting the tile floor like a melon. Thonk. Not only were "cocktails" of gin, Scotch, and bourbon big time, but liquors such as Drambuie,

Grand Marnier, and Cointreau were regularly quaffed, usually after dinner. Wine was not so much in vogue in those days.

Dave and I regularly played after caddying on those summer days, and as we were coming up number 18 at dusk, Keith Myrick's trumpet floated out over the grass. Keith and Abby Green, who played the piano and organ for years there, were fine musicians, passing the critical ear test of my mother, who did not suffer poor musicianship quietly. Diners on the terrace could watch the sun set over the Siskiyou Mountains. I thought it was the good life, and in many ways, it was.

Old Dad Lewis smoked cigars. He lit up, puffed his way down the fairway, tossed the stogie down to hit his shot, retrieved it after handing the club back to me, and strode on. One day, he accidentally picked up a specimen he had thrown down on a previous day, soggy from the sprinklers, and crammed it in his mouth. We dared to laugh, and he did too when he finished spitting. It seemed as if every golfer smoked, usually cigarettes, and while to this day I dislike cigarettes indoors, the smell outside triggers fond memories.

Golf can be played for decades only to produce the realization that you know nothing about the game—it is too deep for you. It will never be your friend. Football great Alex Karras said, "My best score is 103, but I have only been playing for fifteen years."

I knew as a kid that the country club was for relaxation, for social life, for having fun. Much of it was in contrast to the decade of the '40s, which was anything but fun. Life was to be lived, and to live was to be happy. Confusing me, however, was why so many of my masters lost their tempers, threw clubs, abused them, swore nonstop, and turned nasty on their playing partners. Nobody played better mad, and a mad player was likely to give me a smaller tip, as if it were my fault.

From a moral standpoint, happiness is one of the quests that is a destination rather than a weigh station toward some other moral goal. Not that we get there. The Declaration of Independence terms it "the pursuit of happiness." To say "I am going to be happy" is a noble goal, but paradoxically, since it is the destination, you will have to do something else to move you toward that goal. Something like helping another—serving in a soup kitchen, building for Habitat for Humanity, or mowing your neighbor's lawn.

Is there a happiness gene? I think so, and I have it, not that I have done anything to deserve it. It can be highly irritating to others. Just as some are afflicted with depression, the reverse is true. For me, it is not the rose-colored glasses, Pollyanna view that deems everything and everybody wonderful, but it is a fundamentally optimistic and positive view of life with all of its foibles and deficiencies.

One way to be happier is to realize that golf is not a game of "perfect." The best score could have been better—a lipped putt, a diabolical bounce, an approach with one club too few. "The average expert player, if he is lucky, hits six, eight, or ten real good shots in a round. The rest are good misses," says early-twentieth-century champion Tommy Armour. People who win make the fewest mistakes. Every champion knows how to get out of trouble, because they know they will get into trouble. They practice from the woods, the sand, the high rough.

Some say that golf is like a love affair. If you don't take it seriously, it is no fun. If you do take it seriously, it can break your heart. That may be said, but I don't believe it. Unless you are trying to make a living playing golf, the less seriously you take it, the more fun you will have and, as a corollary, the better you will play. Let's face it: life is not perfect. We all make mistakes. The law calls it negligence. Golf calls it shanks, chunks, slices, hooks, tops, whiffs, 4 putts, yips, dubs, airmails, worm burners, 404s, and that is just on the front nine. Humiliation defines the game.

There are lots of life lessons here, one being that mistakes breed mistakes. I hit my drive in the woods, but there was this space, about three feet wide between the trees, and if I could just snake it through there to the green. Three shots later, I am still in the woods. Remember the Clintons and Whitewater? Had they come clean at the beginning, it would have been over. Instead they let it dribble out, mistake after mistake until it became a lasting big deal—a scandal that defines them for history even though most people couldn't tell you what happened. It is a political lesson that is, apparently, unlearnable.

A second lesson is patience. Good golfers have bad memories; they block out the bad shot immediately and patiently plan for the next. A metaphor is the Chinese bamboo tree. You water it for four years, and nothing happens. In the fifth year, it grows ninety feet in six months. Practice is like that sometimes (I mean, surely practice has helped others even if it is a pain in the ass), but the main lesson for pro golfers and for life is "what's next?" What's done is done. Nothin' you can do about it, and if you try, it will get worse. What's next is a new day.

Willie Nelson, the country music-singing golf nut with the par 23 hole in his backyard, has a song about this, not surprisingly entitled "Nothing I Can Do About It Now."

The pre-shot routine is about patience. Pros do it religiously; most amateurs don't think they need to. I once saw Tiger Woods with an insanely difficult chip. Fluff Cowan, his then caddie, noticed that Tiger was distracted by gallery noise and said, "Start over, Tiger." He did. He stepped away, looked at it from all angles, took his practice swings, cleared his mind, and hit it stiff.

It may be a stretch, but this is analogous to twentieth-century philosopher John Dewey's view that ethics is a process, an evolution engaged in broadening the collective good. The metaphysical ideas of truth, beauty, justice, and the like are woven into the everyday fabric of our lives, and by that familiarity they become more meaningful. Ethics is about enabling more people to live the good life, and democracy is the form of government that best allows that to happen. You don't need me to tell you that democracy is something less than perfect, but the point is that we have to be patient with ourselves and our government. Things happen slowly and imperfectly. As long as we keep the moral aspiration, we will muddle through.

John Frohnmayer

CHAPTER 9

Perfect

"Give me ambiguity or give me something else."

—Anonymous

News flash: golf is unfair. A perfect shot can hit next to the pin and back up into the water. You hit a crisp shot to twenty feet, and your opponent skulls a wedge that bounces off the lip of the trap and rolls to six inches from the pin. The wind can be ill-tempered and ugly. Sand can give you a fried egg lie or a peek-a-boo. Balls can skip across water, bounce out of or into the woods, or disappear. Does this sound a lot like life? It is no wonder that golf club manufacturers advertise their clubs as being "forgiving." Religion has no monopoly on the need for second chances. After plunking one in the hazard, dropping it twice, and placing it on the bank, Ricky Fowler was up on the green, looking things over, when the ball decided to roll back into the water. Another stroke penalty.

Control. The swing has so many moving parts: the grip, the takeaway, the turn, the pause at the top, the hands, arms, and elbows on the downswing, the position of the head, the knees and the butt for power, the weight shift for follow-through. You can break down the swing into forty-seven different functions, and if you do, you will hit nothing but chunks and grounders. Golf is a game of rhythm and feel, and if your mind is working on the forty-sixth part of the swing while it is going on, you have no chance. If you are going to practice, practice smooth. Smooooth. Some say that only two things matter in the golf swing: the grip and the stance. Humankind being what it is, that isn't going to dissuade most of us from overanalyzing everything else.

Happiness and success in life have a lot to do with figuring out what we can control and concentrating on that. Theologian Reinhold Niebuhr's famous prayer is "God grant me the serenity to accept the things I cannot change, courage to change the things I can, and wisdom to know the difference."

Pissed off is the default state for many golfers, and there are reasons aplenty. Slow players ahead. Annoying playing partners who insist on explaining what happened on every shot. Players who don't know the rules of etiquette, so they walk in your line, won't let you play through, leave divots in the green. Poor sand trap maintenance. Too much alcohol, too many bruised egos, too many lookups, too many shattered dreams.

One thing I know for sure is that those ever-present golf carts have ruined the sport. I was walking up to hit a few balls before I quit the game tonight and three times—THREE TIMES—I almost got run over by suckfish in three separate carts that came charging at me full speed, brodied around after the dust off, and slammed to a stop with an overtestosteroned pilot who, in the world of competitive sport, couldn't zip up his fly. What happened to walking? What happened to thinking about the next shot as you walked up the fairway? What happened to getting some goddamned exercise?

Oh, and by the way, when I safely reached the practice range, I managed to hit half a dozen nice high-floating 8-irons, and I probably won't quit the game until tomorrow. And also by the way, a briskly walking foursome gets around the course faster than a foursome in carts unless it is one of those courses where the next tee is in a different time zone from the last green.

One more thought on perfect is that servers and others who deal with the public have taken to responding "perfect" to every exchange. "I'll have fries and a Coke." "Perfect." "I'm leaving for Antarctica, never to return." "Purr-fect." "My Gramma is out there sitting in the snow." "Perfect." It has replaced "no problem," which used to be "you're welcome," which used to mean that the persons speaking were paying attention to what was coming out of their mouths. Call me a curmudgeon, but precious little in our society is perfect, and it sure as hell isn't fries and a Coke.

CHAPTER 10

Role Models

"One advantage of bowling over golf is that you
seldom lose your ball."

—BOWLING GREAT DON CARTER

The "old boys" were Alfred Carpenter, Leonard Carpenter, Gene Thorndyke, and maybe one other I am forgetting. They were, well, old. Of course, when you are ten, everyone over twenty seems old, but these men were slow and stooped and hit their drives about 150 yards. Their bags were pencil thin, some clubs had hickory shafts, and they paid a buck per nine. As one of the youngest caddies, I drew their number more often than not, and since they showed up late morning and played slowly, my chances of getting an afternoon job were slim.

The Carpenter brothers were scions of the Rogue Valley. Rumor had it that they were in on the ground floor of IBM and had migrated from New England with fortunes that they invested in pear orchards. Each had a whole hill for his house, and both talked with an accent that spoke of cultivation and privilege. They were pleasant, I was quiet, and occasionally they would give me a golf ball. It didn't take much to keep me happy in those days.

What I remember most vividly is that notwithstanding their collective name, they were treated with respect, admiration, and even a kind of communal love. They were our old boys, and they had chosen us—that is, Medford, Ashland, and the Rogue Valley—to spread their wealth and culture. I don't mean they burst forth with the triumphal chorus from Aida, but they were different in kind from the ordinary golfer—talked about different things, valued different experiences, supported important civic projects. They had what some call "bottom." They had substance. They weren't frivolous. Everything they did and said told me that.

There were plenty of others with whom to compare. Some were full of themselves and their place in this small pond. "The louder they talked of their honor the faster we counted our spoons" (Ralph Waldo Emerson). Honor is a macho sinkhole. Honor provokes duels, fights, even war. Protecting the "honor" of Southern womanhood (read white male insecurity) led to innumerable lynchings. Honor, if it exists, requires no protection, for it is the unassailable character of everything a person is and does.

The Greek philosopher Heraclitus tells us that a man's character is his fate, so let's talk cheating. I was a naïve kid, but I knew when adults were cheating. Here are a few examples. One man would mark his ball in front rather than in back. When he replaced the ball, it was as much as six inches ahead of the coin. He laughed to me that if he could mark it a couple more times, it would be a gimme. A proud cheater. Not one but many players would hit a putt or chip within a reasonably short distance of the cup, say four feet and in, walk up, and pick up the ball, giving themselves the putt when it was nowhere near being "inside the leather." Lots of them would improve their lies in the rough.

None of these were indictable offenses, but all reflected on honor and character. What was I to think? They didn't care what I thought. There was a guy—I don't remember his name because if I did, I would print it here in bold letters—who missed a short putt, buried his putter to the hilt in the green, and stalked off, leaving me to retrieve the putter and repair the green as best I could. I should have left it there.

I suspect there was some price to be paid for cheating, primarily that others wouldn't want to play with that person, but I never saw that part of the dynamic. I did see that the other players in the group would not call out a cheater. I never saw it happen, and I saw plenty of cheating. I was left to ponder whether cheating was the norm, whether it mattered, and what these guys did in the other parts of their lives—in business, with their wives and their friends.

About this time, vice presidential candidate Richard Nixon gave his "checkers" speech. He had been called out for a slush fund his backers created for political expenses. He said he would not give back a gift dog his children had named Checkers. He attacked his accusers and urged the television and radio audience to keep him on the ticket. This was a new kind of public mea culpa. The message was "I am not sorry about what I did, I am only sorry I got caught, and look at all those guys over there who should be punished for other stuff." Ike put his arm around him and called him "son."

There is something called the "Mama rule." If you are afraid to tell it to Mama, you shouldn't be doing it. Good advice. I took the cheating I saw home for discussion at the dinner table and got a dose of old-time religion from my mother. Dad too. We didn't cheat, didn't lie. Those were rules to live by, and they weren't negotiable.

Much later in life, I was travelling around the country talking about First Amendment issues at over one hundred colleges and universities and only two, Brigham Young and a nearby community college, both in Utah, required an ethics course for all students. We make drivers study traffic laws and practice driving before obtaining a license, but we assume we can live well together with no formal instruction on how to treat each other.

Back to the old boys. They were my role models on the course. It wasn't athletic prowess but character that impressed me. Here is my analysis from the mind of an adult and the memory of a child. The good life, the life worth living, must have some element of self-sacrifice, some other direction, some charity and selflessness.

Plato's *Republic* makes the distinction between a life of virtue (service to others) and a life that is good for the person living it. Modern philosopher Patrick Grim calls the first the admirable life and the second the enviable life. To him, the core must be made of virtue with fringes of self-satisfaction such as family, fame, wealth, and play.

Ben Franklin would ask at the end of the day whether he had been a good boy. Life is a moving target. So is morality with everyday challenges, opportunities, failures, and dilemmas. With one's free time is it better to be on the golf course or volunteering at the library? Depends on everything else going on in your life, and chances are your mother isn't going to make that decision for you.

One thing is certain: Life, like golf, is about recovering from bad shots.

CHAPTER 11

Dealing with Stupid

"Golf is a game where you yell fore,
shoot six, and write down five."

—Paul Harvey

The caddie is the on-field coach for the golfer. It is the only sport I know of where the father confessor, cheerleader, humorist, shrink, and Sherpa is right there with the player for every shot. Caddie may derive from the French word *cadet* or from some mossy Scottish notion of an errand runner, but caddies seem to be as old as the game itself. They have their own lingo: "He pulled out a WMD and hit it into the 404." Translation: He hit a 3-wood and hooked it so far out of bounds that it was a file not found. When a caddie says, "my man hit an Oscar Bravo," that means out of bounds (using military letter designations). A "Nancy Pelosi" is a ball to the left, and a "Rush Limbaugh" is to the right. Professional caddies are called loopers.

Caddie stories abound. The caddie laid down the clubs behind the car, and the player backed over them. He undid the strap and pulled the clubs along like a dog sled. He got bumped on the bridge, and the clubs slid out kerplop, kerplop, kerplop into the water. He was drunk and therefore can be excused for saying after the fourth ball into the gorse, "If you pull out that driver again, I will break it."

"Caddie, can I carry the bunker?" "I don't think so, sir. There's ten ton of sand in it."

"I call my player Ray Ray. One day he plays like Ray Floyd and the next like Ray Charles."

"The wind was so strong, there were whitecaps in the porta potty."

"The best wood in the bag is his pencil."

"I've seen better swings in a ghetto playground."

Player: "I've a notion to jump in the pond and drown myself." Caddie: "I don't think you could keep your head down that long."

Silver screen actor Errol Flynn's caddie always worked barefoot, so when Flynn hit it in the rough, he could pick it up with his extra-long toes and deposit it in the fairway. I played barefoot some as a kid, and it was fun so long as you stayed in the fairway and didn't get stung by a bee.

Caddies provide information—yardages, advice (yes, a 6-iron with a slight draw), and help keep it light for the player, particularly one who is in contention when the vice-like pressure builds in the final holes of a tight tournament. As Jack Nicklaus said, "The most important six inches in golf are between your ears." The caddie, with gentle humor, a wise suggestion, or by being steady and quiet, can often save the player from himself.

By the rules, the caddie is the only one who can legally provide advice to the player during a competitive round. Likewise, the caddie's infraction of the rules counts against the player, so when the caddie tending the pin is urging his player's ball to the hole and the tee behind his ear falls into the path of the ball, it's a two-stroke penalty.

A story made the news in 2018 about a seven-hole course in Seneca, Oregon, where they had goats as caddies. They were equipped to carry clubs, balls, and drinks, but I wouldn't be asking a goat about club selection. No way.

Stupid is not new. Historian Barbara Tuchman said of Philip II of Spain, "No experience of the failure of his policy could shake his belief in its essential excellence." He was annoyed with Queen Elizabeth over the maritime exploits of Sir Francis Drake and felt it his moral duty to restore England to Catholicism. He sent out the Spanish Armada in the firm belief that a miracle from God would return victory, and it was crushed. There is no accounting for stupid, and there is no shortage of it either.

Under Presidents Truman, Eisenhower, Nixon, Kennedy, and Johnson, the United States paid little heed to the whipping Ho Chi Minh and General Vo Nguyen Giap gave the French in 1954 after eight years of struggle in Vietnam, so we sucked ourselves in one tar baby hit at a time. We learned nothing from the Soviet incursion into Afghanistan, and after seventeen years, we may never get out. Looking back into history—well, it is as Harry Truman said: "The only thing new in the world is the history you don't know yet." You'd think we would learn not to spit into the wind. Dogma is the enemy of freedom, and pretension is a source of evil. We are the United States, but that doesn't mean we know best for every other country.

How do we deal with stupid? First of all, is it contagious? The answer is yes. Confirmation bias is the phenomena where we hear and believe only that which supports what we already think. Multiple studies show that even after people have been shown that what they relied on is false, they continue to hold the same belief. Electronic platforms from our smartphones to television allow us to silo our information. You can get your news from Pat Robertson, Rachel Maddow, or Daffy Duck, and a lot of folks don't bother to evaluate what they cram in their ears.

Growing up, in those three-hour dinners on the summer patio, Dad would dispatch one of us to get the *World Book Encyclopedia* and look something up when we had a factual impasse. We can do it now with a touch of our phones, and I don't know if that has made us smarter or dumber. We learned to defend our position, to get our intellectual ears boxed, and to value facts. Today, facts seem to be what the speaker wants them to be. Truth is in the dumpster, and a lot of people don't seem to care. No democracy can survive without a commonly accepted understanding of what is true. No democracy can survive without trusted and reliable news sources. The oxymoron of "fake news" is the pablum of morons. The great jurist Learned Hand said, "The spirit of liberty is the spirit which is not too sure it is right." When we cease to be persuadable, we are ideologues, and ideology is the enemy of reason, justice, and a moral universe. When we are too lazy to determine for ourselves what the facts are and what reasonable conclusions can be drawn from those facts we are, well, stupid. Ralph Waldo Emerson said, "Thinking is the hardest work in the world. That is why so few of us do it." It is almost as if we enjoy being conned.

This is cosmically depressing, you might say, but what does it have to do with golf? In the 1968 Masters Tournament, Argentine pro Roberto De Vicenzo's card was being kept by his playing partner, Tommy Aaron. Aaron had written down a 4 for De Vicenzo on number 17 when he had actually scored a 3. De Vicenzo signed the card and lost the tourney for which he had the lowest score. His response was, "What a stupid I am."

PART II

Family Reflections

CHAPTER 12

A Decade of Quiet Turmoil

"You can't shoot an idea with a gun."

—Thomas Dewey,
debating Harold Stassen in the
1948 presidential primary

Context is important, and the 1950s were a time of great plasticity, notwithstanding an even-keeled president and an aura of placid satisfaction. In 1957, Sputnik delivered the message that we were behind the Ruskies in science.

Elvis Presley sold sex and rebellion with every gyration. He learned from James Dean and Marlon Brando never to smile while he was breaking hearts by the boatload. Young people had the money to buy *Hound Dog*, *Don't Be Cruel*, and *Heartbreak Hotel*. He was an industry and a revolution all wrapped up in big hair, pegged trousers, and white socks. Leonard Bernstein called him "the greatest cultural force in the twentieth century."

In Brown v. Board of Education, the Supreme Court told us that separate but equal was inherently unequal. J. Edgar

Hoover, he who had brought down bank robber John Dillinger, was there to rule the FBI and keep us safe, and the H-bomb tested on Bikini Atoll was one thousand times more powerful than that dropped on Hiroshima.

Hugh Hefner served up *Playboy* and the expectation of young men that their new wife would have a staple in her navel. The pill? Well, the pill was the pill, the Catholic Church notwithstanding. McDonalds promised a night off for Mom when the whole family could chow down on fries and shakes for only a few bucks. Ed Sullivan dished out pop stars in three-minute segments on Sunday night as we all sat before our new color sets. Drive-in movies were great for necking and sneaking in a trunk full of friends.

I graduated from caddying to working as a box boy at the Big Y Supermarket. This was the only supermarket in the valley, and I loaded groceries in the used boxes that deliveries came in. After I wedged a few of these into the back seats of sedans, I felt like the Tom Lehrer song about Wernher von Braun's rockets: "Once the rockets go up, who cares where they come down, that's not my department says Wernher von Braun." One time I carried a box about a half mile down the road for a man who had misjudged a slow-moving freight car at the cost of his right leg. I refused all tips.

I also turned down a football scholarship to Stanford. This was Dad's doing. He said we could afford to pay for it ourselves, and the money should go to someone else. Okay, but as I wrote that first quarter's tuition check for $400, I was thinking that this was my caddying money, and it sure better be worth it.

Mother, the worrier, would sit up waiting for me to get home from a date, Bible on her lap. Her greatest fear (next to one of us boys getting a girl pregnant) was that we would marry a Catholic. She was as hung up on sex as the Mother Superior and the Legion of Decency put together. All of this seems hopelessly quaint now, but as much as my father was the head of household and the presumed role model, I absorbed more in the way of music, culture, and humor from my mother. The worrying, the Bible, and the fear of all things Catholic—those faded away like the dreams of a subpar round.

There were many things we as Americans were certain of in the '50s. We were a force for good in the world. Communism, even a hint of it, was bad, and therefore any social or political force opposed to Communism was worth supporting. We had the right to enforce our will by force and, of course, we were, individually and collectively, exceptional. The towering theologian Reinhold Niebuhr said of Eisenhower's Secretary of State John Foster Dulles, "Self- righteousness is the inevitable fruit of simple moral judgments."

Our moral blindness about race became more difficult to ignore, not because we had a sudden upwelling of conscience but because as a society, we cared more about sports than most anything else. Jackie Robinson in baseball, Jim Brown in football, and Bill Russell in basketball were too good to miss.

Eisenhower, his reputation as being mild-mannered and quiet notwithstanding, was full of wisdom. Read his writings, his speeches. They are worth your time. He said, "When you are in any contest, you should work as if there were—to the very last minute—a chance to lose it. This is battle, this is politics, this is everything."

After I had struggled through the first and second grades, my parents concluded that I couldn't read. They had a comparison, since my older brother, Dave, at a precociously infantile age, tore himself from the maternal breast to devour books instead. They sent me to a tutor during the summer to learn phonics. Perhaps I got better, but I remember my third grade teacher chortling that someone wrote that Gitche Gumee was Hiawatha's father—ho ho.[2] All those Indian names confused me, blinded me even, I couldn't see them on the page, and Longfellow has ever after been off my list. Another time we were reading aloud about the Spanish exploration of the Southwest, and I kept getting Coronado and Colorado mixed up until she told me to sit down.

Piano lessons? Never would bother to read the music. I could hear it and play it by ear, but easily discouraged and longing to run around outside, I quit after a year or so. Mother told me I would be sorry, and for a lifetime, I have been.

All this changed. My senior year in high school, I was All Conference in football, State Scholar Athlete of the Year, won the Kiwanis Choir Award and the Elks Leadership Award, sang the lead in the school musical, *Oklahoma*, and went on to excel in a profession in which reading is a critical skill, i.e., lawyering.

What happened? Where does confidence come from, and do morality and confidence have any connection? Is a failure a failure because it happened or because it failed to produce a response? What prompts the gray cloak of regret or the watery-eyed determination that shakes off the mud and shame? One answer is that Medford, in those days, had

---

2   Ojibwa name for Big Water, Lake Superior. The lake could have been his spiritual father, but she was correct in observing that I was totally clueless.

an excellent school system with able, dedicated, and well-financed teachers. Another is that I had siblings who were excelling and parents who cared.

What tools does one need for moral education as opposed to education generally? Morality can and does exist without literacy, but the written word has been preferred since the Ten Commandments. The moral lessons I learned early were visual and aural—for example, watching and hearing adults on the golf course. Are those I learned later from books different?

If there were an answer to how ethics and moral conscience develop, we would have stopped asking these questions thousands of years ago. The main goal is to have a plan, to have thought about the issues before we find ourselves in the midst of them. Chances are the plan will go out the window the minute things get sticky or confusing, but a lot of ethics is like grenades or horseshoes—close is good enough.

Like golf, we can't practice morality until we have decided what we need to practice on and how to go about it. Teacher Harvey Penick said Ben Crenshaw was such a natural golfer that when Crenshaw was young, he didn't encourage him to practice too much for fear he would learn how to do some things wrong.

With morality, we need a role model and a legitimate desire to learn how to do the right thing for the right reason. We need to visualize ourselves in difficult situations, consider the less-than-perfect alternatives, and parse out what response is best. It is called practice, rehearsal, training, education, preparation.

CHAPTER 13

Cars and Trucks

"We only use 10 percent of our brains. Think what we could do if we used the other 60 percent."

—ELLEN DEGENERES

J ust like you don't consciously know you are learning a language as an infant, you also don't know that you are creating a framework for absorbing and using information from which to form a worldview. Family is the primary teacher. If you are lucky enough to have a good family and good parents, your journey through life will be greatly enhanced. I had great parents. All siblings have different parents (I just counted the words in that phrase because I swiped it from Delia Ephron), but I was also fortunate to be the third child: the peacemaker, the comic.

As a subordinate sibling, you get experienced parents who are less likely to hover. You get siblings to admire, like my sister, Mira, who was so funny, so gifted in music and sports, and my brother, Dave, who could outread, outthink, and outtalk all of us. Persuasion was highly prized as was the luxury of being persuadable.

A major conflict between golf and culture arose on a family trip to Victoria, British Columbia. We were staying in the lofty, snooty, and elegant Empress Hotel, but we had packed our golf clubs (I was the designated packer of the car trunk). Dad, Mira, Dave, and I went to play one of the many wonderful courses there not to return in time for high tea, and was Mother annoyed. Totally angry to tears. High tea at the Empress was a big deal with a string quartet playing Vivaldi and Bach, pastries and cakes of indescribable lushness, and of course, tea made as only the English can make it. It was one of the few times I saw her that mad. She had her priorities, and music and style were at the top of the list. I am sure I remember more about high tea—what I have made up and subsequently learned—than if we had dutifully paraded down in a timely fashion.

The driving vacation of the 1950s was a test of whether the kids in the car could drive their parents nuts. In 1953, all six of us drove as far east as Detroit, Michigan. I had to sit in the middle of the back seat (the least favored position) as a buffer between Dave and Phil. All Dave (the older) had to do was sing a few bars of "Slow boat, oh, slow boat," and Phil would fly into a rage, fists gyrating and blows landing mostly on me.

Several years later, we started out in a fancy 1957 Lincoln that had the obligatory tail fins, two-tone turquoise-green-with-cream top, and two over-and-under headlights, the lower set activated by a switch on the steering column. The first part of the trip was dreamy with only Phil (five years my junior), me, Mom, and Dad. Dave was to be picked up in Boston, and Mira would fly to join us when she finished college in Eugene.

About Salt Lake, we began smelling sulfur and declared Utah to be stinky. Stinky everywhere. Turns out we brought the stink with us in the form of a battery located under the front passenger footwell that was crying for water and thankfully not exploding. Service station attendants still looked under the hood in those days. One tumbled to the fact that there was no battery there, leading to a stem-to-stern search and, as a last resort, a consultation of the owner's manual.

We got to Boston and collected Dave, got to Washington and fetched Mira along with some patriotic souvenirs, and headed for White Sulfur Springs, West Virginia. Otto (Dad) knew it was the home course of Sammy Snead: The Greenbrier, an iconic treasure right up there with those in the nation's Capitol.

Otto was at the wheel, the second set of headlights on in the dusk light as we slowly climbed a two-lane mountain road behind a laboring truck. The truck pulled over at the top to let us by. Toot, toot, thanks, and off we go. A few turns later, the bright lights and engine roar announced that the truck was back but not very far back—virtually in our trunk. He had gears and engine braking, and he knew the road. We were terrified. Otto's hair was standing on end as he hunched over the wheel. I have never seen that since, the hair standing straight up and catching the glare of the truck's lights. Turn after turn we gained a little ground, and he came roaring back, threatening to bump us into oblivion.

We survived. Perhaps he was pissed because of our brights, maybe he was just funnin' the out-of-state rubes. It made our arrival at the stately southern and lovely Greenbrier at White Sulphur Springs memorable. First time I had seen white silicone sand in traps. Rogue Valley Country Club bunkers had a mixture of river sand and mud—hard to excavate with a wedge.

Here is one takeaway. The trucker could have made his point with one or two roar-ups. Instead, he did it on every curve for what seemed to us an eternity (literally and figuratively). It is like, but different from, my barn cat, George, throwing a vole into the air, then feigning loss of interest, then pouncing, toying, tormenting, playing. Human cruelty is intentional cruelty. That truck driver had the power to threaten us, to scare us. What did he get out of it? Did he feel powerful, noble, vindicated? Did he go home and describe his exploits to his family?

Since our ethical self emerges and sometimes surprises us with guilt or remorse, how do these sneak up on us? If the truck driver reviewed his actions and felt proud or sorry, would that be a sign of an ethical conscience? To me, his not giving it a second thought would be the most troubling response.

CHAPTER 14

Lessons of the '50s

"TV allows people who don't have anything to do to watch people who can't do anything."

—FRED ALLEN, 1940s radio host

The process of growing up and starting to become educated is deciding what one does well (or could, with adequate training, do well) and what is out of reach. A United States senator I know says he wanted to be a professional basketball player but, upon rigorous self-analysis, realized he was too small, too slow, and his feet too glued to the court. Moral as well as physical education may come at a time when we are more or less ready to be receptive. Like seeds—too early, they freeze; too late, they wither.

My summer world of the '50s consisted of my parents, my older sister, and older and younger brothers, Sunday school where perhaps the most memorable event was Ken Durkee slugging me in the stomach, Vacation Bible School, which I hated, and listening to *The Green Hornet, Dimension X, The Lone Ranger*, and *Inner Sanctum* on the radio at night. I knew, in a vaguely troubling way, that we could all be vaporized by a nuclear blast, but I don't remember ever having to crawl under my school desk, and I didn't spend a lot of emotional energy worrying about it.

A couple of kids who seemed to be everywhere I was weren't especially mean—just arrogant, entitled, and mouthy. Cousins, a year older than I, they had anointed themselves as being in charge of everything, so when I went to get a drink of water at summer baseball (which I also hated), Tony said, "Here is a kid aching for a drink that hasn't even played yet." I shrunk back, duly chastised because I hadn't played, and if I had, I was no hit, no throw, no speed—bereft of baseball skills.

In tackle football in the fifth grade (yes, Medford got into the body crashing early), the coach was Chief McLean (yes, he was a Native American, and yes, everybody called him Chief, but at least that wasn't as bad as a fellow Navy officer I knew years later who called a sailor of Native American lineage "blanketass"). Chief showed me the proper stance for a down lineman with a three-knuckle claw in front, head up, tail down, legs spread, and I stayed frozen that way as he went down the line, not knowing what else to do. When he came back up the line, he said, "This man knows football. Go get a uniform," so I trotted to the equipment room to find Tony and his cousin, Peter, giving me the stink-eye and daring me to take one of the prized Notre Dame type helmets, which I didn't because I was a lowly fifth grader who didn't know squat.

I don't remember learning anything from Tony and Peter except to keep my mouth shut. I did catch a pass playing for Chief the next year. I was totally in the clear behind all defenders on my way to a touchdown, and I tripped and fell down. He couldn't believe it, kept shaking his head and saying, "No one near him, and he falls down." Several years later, I saw Tom Hamlin roar full speed into a blocking dummy, and I thought, "That's the way it is done."

Lessons, to be useful, must be ripe, like a tomato. Playing golf for hundreds of rounds, millions of swings, and suddenly an epiphany: *If I roll my left hand over a little...* That epiphany may last for a few days or a lifetime. The moral revelations and the forward steps build on what we have done and learned before. The changes are usually incremental. Harvey Penick says, "When I tell you to take an aspirin, I don't mean the whole bottle."

The occasional reminder that it was a dangerous world in the '50s was the flyovers of the lone B-36 bomber—the Convair "Peacemaker"—up there at 40,000 or maybe as much as 55,000 feet, cruising along at 423 miles per hour. Those babies had six pusher propellers (and later, four jet engines, "six turnin' and four burnin'"), over 28,000 horsepower, a 230-foot wingspan, and a range of 10,000 miles. We knew they carried nukes and that we could lay some whoop-ass on the Russians if necessary. What was so cool was that the slow-turning propellers interacted with the high-pressure airflow from the wings to produce a low throbbing on the ground. I could hear it (feel it, really), look up, find it in the sky, and feel swell about the whole deal.

Mother was scared to death that we would get polio, and it wasn't until mid-decade when we got the sugar cube with a drop of blue liquid on it—the Salk vaccine—that we were safe. Before that, it was like waiting for a forest fire to break out, and every swim, every chill, every crowded place gave her the worries. She was a champion worrier.

Senator Joe McCarthy was busy rousting out the 208 phantom communists in the State Department, but all I remember about that is…well, I don't remember it at all. I do remember that Dad was part owner of a grocery store, The Big Y. He told us that one of his partners was going on about "the Jews" only suddenly to tumble to the fact that their third partner was, indeed, Jewish. The guy sputtered something like: "I don't mean you, Sam" and remembered an important meeting he had to get to. Medford, despite its many virtues, was a white enclave that had been, and maybe still was, a sundown town.

At the Big Y, you could buy everything from trousers to mayonnaise. I matriculated there from caddying when I was fifteen. First thing each day I was to get a bucket of warm water and a Brillo pad and scrub down the conveyor belts that brought the groceries to the checker. There was a sign painter who, with an artistic flair, painted the specials on butcher paper. The store gave away carnival glass bowls—something for nothing that brought them running.

I was particularly smitten with a Marilyn Monroe-type bleached blonde who worked in the store. I only got rare glimpses of her, and one day, I saw her driving a black Jaguar XK150 with the top down. She was the model of adolescent fantasy. I, on the other hand, was all hat and no cattle—a bewildered gawker.

A rite of passage, I suppose, was Colleen Hope's dance classes. We dressed up in blue blazer and tie, got ferried to the country club where over ten lessons, we learned the box step, got our hair parted from the breath of the girls who were all taller, had a Coke and a hamburger, and were duly socialized. Colleen was just what you imagine: bleached blond, black, slinky dress with feather boa, cigarette breath, and scary.

There was a war going on in Korea. MacArthur, so heroic at Inchon, got his heinie kicked at the Yalu, and Matthew Ridgeway quietly saved the day. Truman fired MacArthur, who richly deserved it, but a master of the metaphor with only a passing acquaintance with the truth, MacArthur came home a hero. I thought he was then. Don't now.

I was busy growing and watching and doing. I went from summer job to summer job, which brings us to an adult named Grace—a misnomer if ever there was one. She was far from my favorite of my parents' friends, but nonetheless, she and her family were part of all the multifamily get-togethers that exemplified the rich social life of a small town in America the Affluent of the 1950s and 1960s.

I was pulling weeds at the hospital. Sunny day. Hot. Grace screeched up in her red-and-white Chevy convertible, top down, and greeted me as I stood there, dumbly, weeds in hand. "John," she said, "I forgot my flat shoes, and I am late for my candy striper (volunteer) duty, so the shoes are on the back porch, and here are the car keys." She hurried off, not waiting for my reply as if a refusal was out of the question. I was working for someone, don't remember who, but it surely wasn't Grace. I don't remember a "please" or, for that matter, Grace giving the tiniest shit about the fact that I was being paid $3.25 an hour to work for somebody else.

I did it. I drove to her house, fetched the shoes, took them to her in the hospital gift shop along with the car keys, received a perfunctory thank you, and returned to the weeds. What should I have done? What did I learn about authority, about ranking obligations, about family friends, about being sucker punched? Why, of all of the incidents of my young life, do I remember this one?

Could I have said no? Now I could. "Grace, I am busy with these weeds, which, if you will notice, are growing like weeds, and if I drive to your house, there will be more weeds when I get back. As you can well imagine, that would be intolerable." Big smile.

It was about power. She was an adult, and I wasn't (although I would have been at least sixteen, because I could drive). She knew I wouldn't push back, because I was polite and she was a family friend. She abused her power. I doubt seriously that she gave it a second thought.

CHAPTER 15

Family Music

"Without music, life would be a mistake."

—FRIEDRICH NIETZSCHE

I f there is one unifying central part of me, as I define myself and as I have lived my life, it is music. My mother played the piano beautifully, taught music, started the "mother singers" in Medford, had perfect pitch, and could play anything by ear (without the aid of written music). She did all of that with only one good ear (rheumatic fever as a child). Two of my siblings (Mira and Phil) had the guts to be professional musicians, and I admire them without ceasing for their courage and success in doing so. Being a classical singer, particularly in America, is no walk in the park.

Music goes back as far as my memory. On Sunday afternoon drives around the Rogue Valley, we sang four-part songs, and you had to learn to hold your own, no matter how loudly your stupid sibling was singing another part in your ear. The living room held two grand pianos. Mira played the viola and the piano; Dave, the trumpet; I, the trombone (much to the dismay of all others who heard me practice) and the guitar; and Phil, the piano, sax, and drums. First and foremost, we were singers. We sang show tunes, Brahms, Hugo Wolf, Christmas carols, school assignments, and anything else we felt like. No family function was without music. When we weren't making it, it was on the record player or the radio. Phil, at age five, wore out the 78 rpm record of the opera *Carmen* so that the hole was elongated and it had a wow in the habanera. Company would arrive, and Father instructed, "Dave, get your trumpet. Mira, your viola." We were expected in music, as in all other aspects of our lives, to perform. I don't remember being asked to get my trombone.

Music brought a lot to the table in an ethical sense. Take, for example, the Pete Seeger song *Turn, Turn, Turn* written in the late fifties and recorded by The Limeliters, The Byrds, and Seeger himself. Judy Collins also sang it, as did Marlene Dietrich, in German. The lyrics are straight from Eccles. 3:1–8: "To everything there is a season and a time for every purpose under heaven." We sang it, listened to it, and wondered whether there should be a time to kill as opposed to a time to heal. Why should we refrain from embracing? A time to love, yes sir, but why a time to hate? Why a time of war, especially if Jesus, the promised one, was called the Prince of Peace? A time to speak and a time to keep silent? I concur, particularly with the silence part.

We sang every hymn in the book, we sang the Messiah, we sang Bach cantatas, Brahms, Mozart, and Faure Requiems, we sang in every choir the church and schools established, and we were blessed with a superb choral conductor and friend in the person of Lynn Sjolund. The words were the words, and if we were singing in Latin or some language with which I was not familiar (which includes all of the world's languages, past and present, save English), it was just what you did to produce the sound. The sound and the rhythm: that was what mattered to me. That was what was beautiful.

Leonard Cohen's song "Hallelujah" that I sing now with my guitar has been recorded by every singer under the sun, k.d. lang's version being my favorite. "I heard there was a secret chord that David played, and it pleased the Lord, but you don't really care for music, do ya?" I don't claim to channel Cohen's thoughts in choosing the words, but every time I sing it, I start to mist up. Maybe I am headed for a moral awakening.

"By the Rivers of Babylon" was recorded by the Melodians in 1972 and is based on Psalms 137. It is a Rastafarian take on oppression and how one can sing the Lord's song in a strange land. It picks up one of my favorite passages from Psalms 19: "Let the words of my mouth, and the meditation of my heart, be acceptable in thy sight, O Lord, my strength and my redeemer." Terrific rhythm.

Another is The Rolling Stones' "Prodigal Son" based on the parable in Luke 15:11–32 where the son says gimme, gimme, gimme, takes off and blows his inheritance, comes back abject, and says he will eat with the hogs, but his father kills the fatted calf and welcomes him with love. The song contains the line "that is the way for us to get along." It is a metaphor for lost and recovered faith and lost and recovered golf balls.

Singing together as we did as a family, in church fellowship, or in any of the dozens of groups with which I have sung since binds us to a common purpose. It allows us to engage each other, to appreciate each other, to recognize the dignity and personhood of each as we strive toward collective action, i.e., to sing whatever music is chosen and to sing it well. Music is a gift from the composer to the world and the performer to the audience.

The term "music appreciation" encompasses far more than being able to distinguish Mozart from Holst. Learning how music is made, how the parts, the rhythm, the words, and the message all fit together is not that distant from learning about and feeling compassion, empathy, and sympathy for others. Beauty connects and nourishes all of them.

Music helps us store life's memories of love and sorrow. After the attacks of September 11 when we as a country were grieving and trying to understand, I found myself playing the second movement of Brahms' Symphony No. 2 over and over on my car stereo. I did it unconsciously at first and then realized that I was comforted by that movement. Still am.

CHAPTER 16

Some Moral Analysis

"If your prayers were always answered, you would
have reason to doubt the wisdom of God."

—Anonymous

American Field Service's summer exchange program
came to our high school in 1957, and my brother
Dave was the first chosen. He went to northern Germany, learned about beer, about fellow students who were
intending to go to Ivy League schools such as Harvard, and
about a world with dimensions vastly broader than the Rogue
Valley. In all respects, the program was a colossal success. It
opened vistas, connected my family with one abroad, and
fostered understanding. We all benefitted, most of all Dave.

Two years later, I was chosen. "You can't go," Mother told
me. "Our family has already had the benefit of this program.
You should decline." I wanted to go in the worst way, not just
to keep up with my brother, but because I knew it could be a
life-changing opportunity. I knew she was right, though, and
I can still see the shock on the face of the teacher who was in
charge of selection when I gave my reasons. Medford was too

small to hog the goodies. My best female friend was chosen, and the experience was as formative for her as it had been for Dave.

How did I feel about it? Ambivalent, that's how. Not noble. Not exactly cheated, because I had no right to it, but that it was an opportunity missed. Would my life have been different? No way of knowing, but it has been pretty darn good. I guess I felt like the second son who doesn't inherit the kingdom so he goes into the priesthood instead.

To say ethics is about right and wrong doesn't get us far. It would have been wrong for me to accept the foreign travel; it was right for me to refuse. So what? If ethics were based solely on ego—what is best for me—I would have accepted and deemed myself ethical in doing so. What if I didn't go and something awful happened to the person who did? What if my refusal caused the sponsors to pull out so no student thereafter could have the experience?

A preferable, although by no means easier, analysis is to look for what is right or for what is good. Utilitarians Jeremy Bentham and John Stuart Mill might argue that the greatest good for the greatest number—maximizing pleasure and minimizing pain—would be the analytical focus, and a greater number of families would benefit from my stepping back. The philosopher Immanuel Kant, on the other hand, would ask, "What is right to do?" One must do the right thing regardless of the consequences. His categorical imperative is that what I choose must be universal—that is, applicable to all persons. Existentialist Jean-Paul Sartre would say that the moral choice I make for myself is for all mankind, and the knowledge of that human connectedness sets me free.

If theories of right and good seem, with a little tweaking, to do a do-si-do and change positions, welcome to the world of philosophy. Most of philosophy is deciding where to start. If you believe in a revealed religion, it could start with the Torah, the Koran, or the New Testament. If you are a naturalist, you might look to the rules of the natural world. American pragmatists say that what works is true; what doesn't, isn't. Once you have set the foundation, which may require a leap of faith, logic proceeds from that premise, and deciding what to do, what to value, becomes clearer. Consistency is a value in ethics so one can extrapolate from one situation to the next, but we are not looking for immutable rules, because no two situations are likely to be exactly the same. We have to be ethically nimble. It is like grooving your golf swing, knowing that you may end up under a tree where you can't use it. We are looking for a usable approach to morals, life, and golf. By thinking about issues and making some personal decisions, we can achieve moral confidence. That is worth a lot. Moral certainty, on the other hand, is far more elusive.

Here is an extraordinary piece of ethical courage I heard recently. Public radio has a series of short conversations meant, I suppose, to reflect on American life. I find the episodes vaguely annoying, but I heard one between a ten-year-old boy and his mother that was astounding. They were talking about safety drills in case a shooter entered the school. He said they were supposed to lock the classroom door, and all twenty-three kids were to stand against the back wall. The teacher was having trouble pushing her desk against the door, so this boy said he helped her.

His mother asked if that was his job, and he said, no, he just saw that she needed help. His mother asked, "Then what?"

"I would stand in front and take a bullet for my classmates."

"I couldn't let you do that."

"Better one dead and twenty-two live."

"What if I told you not to? I want, I need you to come home."

"I would do it anyway."

What an astonishing exchange. We were told nothing about the boy or his family or at least nothing I heard. What kind of training or experience in his tender years would have prompted such selflessness? Would he have had the same conversation with his classmates? Had he witnessed heroics in others, read of such exploits, practiced this scenario in his head?

Sure, our society is sick when people with guns attack the most vulnerable, but here is a child who decided life is for living, and he was willing to give up his for others. I hope he never has to, because he is the citizen we all wish we could be.

CHAPTER 17

Belonging

"Good people sleep better than bad people, but
bad people enjoy being awake more."

—Woody Allen

While the '50s were supposedly a decade of youth
rebelling, what with James Dean, rock 'n roll, Elvis,
and all, I never saw any need to. By my way of thinking, anything I wanted was available. I don't mean for free but
for a modest price, a minimal amount of work, or asking nicely.

Want a car? One day, Dad came home with a 1951 red
Ford convertible with a continental kit on the back. It had
air horns mounted on the front fenders that I immediately
removed, but with the obligatory loud pipes and an even
brighter new red paint job, it was cherry.

New golf clubs, clothes, musical instruments—there wasn't
much we asked for and didn't get. What did we give in return?
We weren't disrespectful, had good manners, both table and interpersonal, got good grades, went to church, cleaned up our rooms.

Didn't I have some obligation to give my parents a hard
time? Why would I do that? I never had the least doubt that

they loved me, wanted the best for me, and what they told me to do was probably in my best interest even if I didn't immediately see it that way. I was still free to ask why it should be done and why I should be the one to do it.

I was almost totally on the reward side of the reward/punishment continuum. Lots of dog training is done like this—tasty treats for heeling, sitting, rolling over, etc. That was me. There wasn't much on the punishment side, such as getting sent to the principal's office (never), getting caught by the police (never), getting my car taken away (once, but it didn't last long because Mom got tired of taking me everywhere), or getting grounded (never). I wasn't sent to my room or given extra chores. I did regularly mow the lawn, clean the pool, sweep the terrace, and rake the leaves, but those were all chores that I didn't exactly enjoy but didn't loathe. In fact, mowing, sweeping, and cleaning have always struck me as having the singular virtue of immediately demonstrating and rewarding your efforts unlike much of the work we do with our heads.

Theories of punishment differ in degree but not in kind from those in the household. Capital punishment (for those who believe in it, and I am not one of them) is justified on grounds of retribution—an eye for an eye—or deterrence—seeing one person executed will prevent others from committing the crime. Deterrence seems ineffectual, since most murders are crimes of passion. Retribution is uncivilized. Throwing away the key is a much better solution, so the person is permanently isolated from society. The added virtue is that the person convicted is still alive when the DNA evidence proves innocence.

Should there be capital punishment in golf? It could be like an Old Testament stoning where the miscreant is tied to a pole and the club members hit golf balls at him. Given the level of expertise, this could take weeks. For what crimes? Driving a golf cart across the green? Peeing in the pool? Probably not a good idea.

The classic Civil War novel *The Killer Angels* by Michael Shaara has a passage toward the beginning, just before the battle of Gettysburg, where an officer from Maine is told to take a group of deserters and deal with them. In the forty seconds it takes him to walk to their compound, he has to decide whether to have them shot, keep them confined, turn them loose, or persuade them to fight. What he says is that we are basically fighting for each other. One hundred and twenty of them choose to fight and hold the flank of Little Round Top. Poor analogy that it is, I think I knew that what I was doing in the family was for all of us. Sure, I was the primary beneficiary but by no means the only beneficiary.

What was going on here was a major infusion of belonging. It is what makes families, street gangs, cults, fighting forces, and nations work. "When you're a Jet, you're a Jet all the way from your first cigarette to your last dying day." So goes the song from *West Side Story.* Two questions arise: Are you locked in to the morality of the group, and to belong, must you necessarily exclude others?

CHAPTER 18

Words Are Just Words

"In the beginning the universe was created. This
has been widely regarded as a mistake."

—DOUGLAS ADAMS

At bedtime, Dad would come in and lie down on Dave's
bed or mine and tell Wally-Wog stories. Wally-Wog
was a fanciful character who got into, and mostly out
of, situations much like young boys such as Dave and John
would encounter. Some of these situations were unresolved
because Dad would doze off mid-sentence and, when prodded
in the ribs, would resume a completely different story that
might or might not tie up loose ends. Such was his imagination, both waking and sleeping.

Then came time for the Lord's Prayer: "Our Father, which
art in heaven, hallowed be thy name. Thy kingdom come,
thy will be done, on earth as it is in heaven. Give us this day,
our daily bread, and forgive us our debts, as we forgive our
debtors. And lead us not into temptation, but deliver us from
evil. For thine is the kingdom, and the power and the glory
forever. Amen."

Like Jeremiah the Bullfrog, I never understood a word he said. Why would our Father need our puny human help to make either his kingdom or his will be done on earth? Is he God or what? Forgiving debts always meant money to me. Did I not owe it if I spent, and why should I give a pass to those caddies who owed me a bunch of golf tees? The big one is why a god would have to be asked to not take us down the dark alleys of bad acting. Finally, if God is God, why does he need us to remind him that his is a swell domain and he is the one with the juice? Amen indeed.

Truth is, I memorized the words, regurgitated them by rote, and thought little about what they meant. Same with the Apostles' Creed (or was it the Nicene Creed?) that we recited every Sunday at church. I recognize now the power of repetition, particularly out loud in a group, but I let myself float along with the wave. It wasn't until I got to seminary in graduate school that I learned how much of what I had declared I believed each Sunday wouldn't bear scrutiny.

Here is monotheism's self-sustaining simplicity: Humankind has fallen—eaten the forbidden fruit—and we live in a soiled state because only a supreme power can change history. God, in Christianity's version, sends his son to be sacrificed. This is a loving God (the New Testament) as opposed to a vengeful God (Old Testament), but the tariff is that humankind must believe in order to be saved. That is the carrot. The stick is that there is a devil and a hell that are, respectively, your master and your destination if you don't believe. Heavy stuff. I prefer Garrison Keillor's quip that we know Adam was a Lutheran, because who other than a Lutheran, when standing next to a naked woman, would be tempted by a piece of fruit?

PART III

Being Churched

CHAPTER 19

What Kinds of Talents?

"Just because nobody complains doesn't mean
all parachutes are perfect."

—BENNY HILL

When I go searching for sources of morality, one would think that church would top the list. Church is where you go for ethics like the grocery store is where you go for food. For me, there were lots of lessons from church, but most of them were ambiguous.

Church was a given on Sunday morning, but getting the family rounded up, fed, and across town was predictably difficult, so we were always late and missed the opening hymn. We cut loose on the second one—five loud musicians and my father who couldn't carry a tune in a bucket but led on in enthusiasm. Counting the turnarounds from other congregants was our favorite part of the service.

Here is a well-known piece of ethical advice that we were taught: the parable of the talents. See what you can make of it, trying, as have I, to see it with fresh eyes as if you are meeting it for the first time. This is recorded in Matt. 25 and

Luke 19 as the words of Jesus, and while the versions differ, the message appears to be the same. A nobleman or lord went on a journey, leaving his servants with his money. Some got more (to every man according to his several ability). When the lord returned, those who got the most had doubled the money with usury (interest), but the one who got the least buried it or wrapped it in a cloth. Those who doubled the money were praised as good and faithful servants, promised authority over the lord's holdings, and invited to share the joy (prosperity) of the lord.

The servant who did not invest, when called to answer, said he knew the lord was a hard (austere) man, that he reaped what he did not sow and took up what he did not lay down, and he (the servant) was afraid. The lord called him a wicked and slothful servant, confirmed that the servant was correct in describing the lord's character, stripped him of the money, and ordered that he be cast out (the Luke version suggests that he could be killed).

Here is the summary message in Matt. 25:29–30: "For unto everyone that hath shall be given, and he shall have abundance: but from him that hath not shall be taken away even that which he hath. And cast ye the unprofitable servant into outer darkness: there shall be weeping and gnashing of teeth."

Granted, it is a parable, a metaphor, and as such, it is susceptible to multiple interpretations, but could the message be that Jesus is commanding us to do the bidding of an avaricious and immoral leader at pain of having our teeth gnashed? Heaven forfend.

The traditional reading, the historical one, is that it is God's pleasure that we make money, and Christian theologians, John Calvin among them, preached that material wealth was a sign of god's favor. What is doubly curious is that usury was forbidden to the Israelites by the Torah (Deut. 23:19–20). Actually, it was forbidden for one's brother but okay for a stranger. Didn't Christ throw the money changers out of the temple?

Some other lessons:

1. You are expected to perform according to the abilities you possess. Karl Marx put this as "from each according to his ability, to each according to his need."

2. There is a hint of evangelism here—if you have the richness of the Word, you must spread it.

3. It is a zero-sum game—what one gets is taken from another.

4. You will be judged.

5. The ruler executes his enemies.

6. Civil disobedience can cost you.

We could continue to ponder these passages, supposedly the unadulterated word of God, but the question inevitably arises: what kind of God is this?

Hot on the heels of Matthew's parable of the talents is the one about the sheep and the goats in Matt. 25:31–46. It was an agrarian society, so the animal characteristics would be well known, but have they changed that much? In Matthew's version, the sheep are put on the right hand of God at judgment day because they gave food, water, and garments when God was imprisoned, and nursed the sick, and for all of that, they are invited to heaven. Goats, on the other hand, didn't do any of these things, so God sentences them thus: "Depart from me, ye cursed, into everlasting fire, prepared for the devil and his angels…into everlasting punishment."

From my observation living on a farm with both goats and sheep, sheep blindly follow each other whether the leader has a destination in mind or not. They run away. They die enthusiastically. They get caught in fences. They are defenseless. Goats, on the other hand, will come to you, sit on your lap, eat your hat, rise up on their hind legs and butt each other, forage, and find food for themselves. They give milk, reproduce efficiently, walk behind you. In short, they are independent, resourceful, and sturdy.

What has God got against goats?

CHAPTER 20

That Pesky Sex Thing

"I am an atheist, and I thank God for it."

—George Bernard Shaw

Here is the Old Testament reading you would *never* see on the reader board at the First Presbyterian Church of Medford: Song of Solomon—any verse. I can hardly imagine the apoplectic seizure my mother would have had if Pastor Kirk/Doctor West, had read, "I am black, but comely...he shall lie all night betwixt my breasts." The sermon based on that reading would have been voluptuously interesting because for the most part, promoters of the faith don't know what to do with King Solomon's highly charged, erotic poetry.

Poetry it is and beautiful:

> *...Rise up, my love, my fair one, and come away.*
> *For, lo, the winter is past, the rain is over and gone;*
> *The flowers appear on the earth; the time of the*
> *singing of birds is come,*
> *And the voice of the turtle is heard in our land.*

Song of Solomon 2:10-12

Granted, Song of Solomon is confusing on multiple levels, gender and voice being two of them. It is Solomon's writing, presumably from somewhere between the tenth and third century BCE, but the first voice—"I am black, but comely"—is feminine and the praise of the female form, masculine. There is the passage "thou hast ravished my heart, my sister, my spouse." What do we do with that? Or with "thy two breasts are like two young roes that are twins, which feed among the lilies"?

This part of the Bible was unknown to me until I was old enough to drink alcohol, not that the two have anything to do with each other, but I suspect if we Americans were a little less hung up on sex, this song, this ode to the beauty of nature and humanity's place in it could have been an inspiration for preserving that beauty rather than despoiling it in pursuit of wealth. To me, the message is that God gets our bodies and our souls. Our passion for each other and our religious experience are enhanced by appreciation of our oneness with the earth. I'll take this narrative over John Calvin's advocacy for money as a sign of God's favor any day.

Rabbi Abraham Heschel makes a similar case for the beauty and spiritual power of music:

"The shattering experience of music has been a challenge to my thinking on ultimate issues...music leads to the threshold of repentance, of the unbearable realization of our own vanity and frailty and of the terrible relevance of God. I would define myself as a person who has been smitten by music."

He believed that music is the soul of language, and nowhere in the Bible is the music and poetic beauty of language more apparent than in the Song of Solomon:

John Frohnmayer

Set me as a seal upon thine heart,
As a seal upon thine arm;
For love is strong as death …
Many waters cannot quench love,
Neither can the floods drown it.

SONG OF SOLOMON 8:6-7

Christianity can be credited for much of the development of Western civilization. It encouraged charities and aid to the poor, but it could have, with equally persuasive reliance on biblical passages, encouraged conservation of the earth's resources, preservation of its beauty, kindness to all living creatures, and peace among peoples of varying beliefs.

I am critical of Christianity on multiple grounds, not the least of which is that it is monotheistic, which means that every other religion is necessarily wrong. It keeps us as children both in its language and in the sense that although we have intellect, we must be spoon-fed religious truth. The reward/punishment, heaven-or-hell dichotomy is meant to scare us straight and is, to me, incompatible with a love ethic. Much of the message is about what we can't do as opposed to human fulfilment. Finally, it encourages us to be selfish about my salvation, my personal relationship with Christ, my being born again.

All of these criticisms can be refuted, but it is still a two-thousand-year-old worldview. I recognize how life-sustaining religion is for those who believe, and I respect that. I grew up with religion, have given it a close look all of my life, and have chosen to take from it those principles that work in my journey toward trying to lead an ethical life. That I haven't taken the whole bundle—well, I have to risk a hot hereafter.

As a belated ante-penultimate thought, Christianity is based on salvation by faith, not works. Faith and forgiveness together constitute a "get out of jail free card," essentially erasing morality (this was Kierkegaard's view). The realm of ethics is about what you do now, here, on earth, in this life. I would put the emphasis on works: saving the planet, feeding the poor, seeking alternatives to war and violence. Those come first. Those are immediate, compelling, and necessary. If you want to believe, that is swell, but pay attention to this life.

CHAPTER 21

The Big Ten

"When people are least sure,
they are most dogmatic."

—JOHN KENNETH GALBRAITH

Exodus 31:18 tells us of the two stone tablets (the lapidary words) written with the finger of God, and Exodus 20: 2–17 contains the text of the Ten Commandments themselves. Commandments means you should pay attention, and these were some moral declarations with which I was familiar as a child. Familiar doesn't mean I understood them.

The first four are God saying give me my due: no other gods before me, no graven images, don't take my name in vain, and keep the Sabbath holy. I thought that was what we did as a matter of course, going to church and all. I got my mouth washed out with soap once for what my mother heard as an ungodly swear word. Once with an Ivory soap rinse was more than enough.

The rest of the commandments are for the ordering of society: honor thy father and mother, don't kill, don't commit adultery (I didn't know what that meant—must be something that adults do), don't steal, don't bear false witness, don't covet your neighbor's wife, servant, ox, etc. Is that it? If there were more, couldn't God have put his finger to work and let Moses and the people of Israel know? How about being kind to each other, helping one another, feeding the poor, and a host of other practices that would make for a just and inclusive society? I mean, if one is going to the trouble to write these in stone, shouldn't they be the foundation of a worthy society? These weren't my thoughts then; I just imagined Moses dragging these heavy tablets down from the mountain. The tablets and the burning bush—those were the things that had presence for me, not what was written on them.

Scholars suggest that some or all of the commandments came from Hittite or Mesopotamian laws, and whether they were off of God's finger or some preliminary pagan source, they do have value for ordering a society. The monotheistic element is probably the most original. Having only one god narrows the field not just of deities but of what that god expects. One doesn't have to deal with the conflicting noise of multiple celestial voices, and once the deity has spoken, it is the word, because there is only one god. This simplifies things but it also becomes the source of eternal conflict. If there is only one god and people are relying on some other source, there will be war.

Years later, that is to say, as an adult, I was practicing law in Bozeman, Montana, and a lower court judge posted the Ten Commandments on the wall behind his bench. A few of us protested that he was injecting religion into the justice system in violation of the First Amendment prohibition against the establishment of religion. He put up the Code of Hammurabi and maybe a picture of Abe Lincoln or some other stuff to show that it was a historical collage rather than a legal requirement. A senior judge saw nothing amiss and thought I was a troublemaker, an unfortunate moniker in a jurisdiction in which there were only two senior judges. What if you were a Buddhist or an atheist and the guy who was judging you had declared, by what was posted on his wall, that you were on the wrong side of the Almighty?

My other question for that judge, which I can ask with impunity now that I am retired from trial practice and don't have to curry his favor, is if I wanted to demonstrate my piety, my belief, my pharisaical ardor, wouldn't some New Testament passages about love, charity, and redemption have more to say to the miscreants who appeared in court?

CHAPTER 22

Proverbial Proverbs

"No one has finer command of the language than
the person who keeps his mouth shut."

—SAM RAYBURN

Proverbs was my mother's favorite Old Testament book. It is full of advice, much of it dated but all of it, according to King Solomon who is giving this advice to his son(s), directly from the Lord. Examples of that advice are as follows:

1. Knowledge is good, as is wisdom. These come from the Lord.

2. Beware of loose women, harlots, and whores who will lead ignorant and impressionable males astray.

3. Sons should listen to their fathers.

4. Keeping your mouth shut is often a good idea.

5. Mercy and truth should be "written upon the table of your heart."

6. If you are wicked, your sins will catch up with you.

Is this book sexist? Does the devil beat his wife? It is surely male-centric, but the son is directed to keep the commandment of his father and forsake not the law of his mother (Proverbs 6:20). Solomon seems to be hung up on wicked women, advising repeatedly to avoid their evil designs, and wickedness generally is an anathema. We get that after about the tenth iteration. Knowledge is good, knowledge is good, knowledge is good. Wisdom too.

Spare the rod and spoil the child, an aphorism recorded in the sixteenth century by Erasmus, comes from Proverbs 13:24. Erasmus compiled a book of aphorisms called *The Adages*, many of which came from the Bible.

"Better is a dinner of herbs where love is than a stalled ox and hatred therewith" (Proverbs 15:16). Later translations use dinner of vegetables and fatted calf or big steak. We now know that the fatted calf will clog our arteries, so the advice is good on multiple levels.

"Pride goeth before destruction, and a haughty spirit before a fall" (Proverbs 16:18). Erasmus picked this one up too, and many of the seven deadly sins are featured prominently in Proverbs. The deadlies, in case you haven't memorized them, are pride, covetousness, lust, anger, gluttony, envy, and sloth. A mnemonic to help you remember them is List Enumerates Character Attributes Guaranteeing Political Success. If that one doesn't float your boat, try Presbyterians Gasp at Sight of Crowds Enjoying Life.

> *"He that is slow to anger is better than the mighty; and he that ruleth his spirit than he that taketh a city."*
>
> —PROVERBS 16:32.

"A false witness shall not be unpunished, and he that speaketh lies shall not escape."

—PROVERBS 19:5.

"Slothfulness casteth into a deep sleep; and an idle soul shall suffer hunger."

—PROVERBS 19:15.

"To do justice and judgment is more acceptable to the Lord than sacrifice."

—PROVERBS 21:3.

Here is just one of the many admonitions about evil women:

"For a whore is a deep ditch; and a strange woman is a narrow pit."

—PROVERBS 23:26.

I like this one:

"Who hath woe? Who hath sorrow? Who hath contentions? Who hath babbling? Who hath wounds without cause? Who hath redness of eyes? They that tarry long at the wine; they that go to seek mixed wines."

—PROVERBS 23:29–30.

You might ask why all these quotes are from the King James Version of the Bible rather one of the dozens of modern translations. It is the King's English, that's why. It is the language of Shakespeare. It is the most poetic, the most beautiful, the most profound example of how we communicate in English.

"Trust in the Lord" is Proverbs' seminal message, but I think it is a mixed message. "Trust in the Lord with all thine heart and lean not unto thine own understanding." Proverbs 3:5. The disconnect is that we are supposed to become educated and wise, and presumably that knowledge will inform our actions rather than fact-free faith. I was sitting in the Veteran's Administration clinic waiting to be called for my appointment when a lady, without preamble, said, "God chose our president. Whoever is elected is God's will." I was revving up to ask her how she knew this when I was called for my appointment. Today, Sarah Sanders, President Trump's spokesperson, said she believes God elected him too. Help me here. Is it God we should blame for this political disaster?

The issue is the problem of evil. How can God, if he/she is involved in the affairs of humankind, stand by while evil flourishes? Philosopher David Hume, in his *Dialogues Concerning Natural Religion,* wrote, referencing the thought of Epicurus:

> *Is he willing to prevent evil, but not able? Then he is impotent. Is he able but not willing? Then he is malevolent. Is he both able and willing? Whence then is evil? Nothing can shake the solidity of this reasoning: so short, so clear, so decisive.*

Hume wrote this the same year as our Declaration of Independence in which Jefferson called upon "Nature's god" to bless the separation of the colonies from King George III. God is convenient when needed and otherwise off busy with other things. To suggest he/she has a hand in the everyday doings of humans denies free will. Either we have the ability to screw up on our own, to harm others, and embrace evil, or God is messing with us.

Hume also wrote "reason is a slave to the emotions," a perception that put him hundreds of years ahead of the neuroscientists of this century.

CHAPTER 23

Commanding Love

"Never do anything virtuous until you minimize
the damage it will cause."

—Edgar Schneider

Learning to love others is the most urgent ethical commandment, but one must first learn to love one's self,
without which love of others isn't possible. Where does
self-love come from? From knowing that you are loved. It is a
conundrum: If you know you are loved, you can love yourself,
but if you don't love yourself, you can't love others. Bummer.
If your parents don't demonstrate that they love you, what
other sources of self-affirmation are there? Siblings—maybe.
Neighbors and strangers—less likely. Can you develop self-
love without outside corroboration? Tough but not impossible.

Because human love is fickle (insert here the lyrics of any
country music song), and because it may not have favored you
from birth, accepting the love of God is attractive, compelling
even. God's love, in Christian theology, resulted in Christ's
sacrifice—no greater love than giving up one's life. The quid
pro quo is that we love God and keep his commandments.

One of those commandments is that we love one another. "A new commandment I give unto you, that ye love one another; as I have loved you, that ye also love one another" (John 13:34). Can love be commanded? If I think you are "a dirty skunk and an ornery pig stealer," as in the lyrics in the musical *Oklahoma!,* must I love you, three dirty shirts and all? How can I be compelled to do so? Isn't love an emotion, a feeling?

Old Testament love was less universal. "Thou shalt not avenge nor hear any grudge against the children of thy people, but thou shalt love thy neighbor as thyself…" (Lev. 19:18). Love your tribe. Foreigners, not so much.

The sort of saint, Paul, gets into the act: "Owe no man any thing, but to love one another: for he that loveth another has fulfilled the law" (Rom. 13:8). This sounds Old Testamentish wherein fulfilling the law took precedence over good sense. Paul also says that loving one another covers a multitude of sins. This suggests love is a useful tool, one that God says we gotta have, but it reads to me as neither loving nor spontaneous—more of like an all-purpose cleanser.

What did I learn about love on the golf course? I could say I love golf for what it taught me about myself, but I could say I hated it for the same reason. Every time I think I have my swing under control, it betrays me. When I start to putt well, my mind sticks in to give me unsolicited advice, and I choke.

Betrayal is fundamental to the Christian message. Judas betrayed Christ with a kiss. Citizens gave false witness about Christ's supposed transgressions and demanded he be crucified even when Pilate found no fault in him and Peter denied three times that he was a disciple (John 18:13–27). The message about betrayal must have filtered into my young brain.

How with all the church, the Vacation Bible School, and home religious instruction could it not have? It was a big-time sin, because it was a breach of trust, a failure of loyalty to a friend, a loved one, a mentor, or a god. As the English philosopher and poet William Blake said, it is easier to forgive an enemy than a friend.

CHAPTER 24

New Wine and Old Bodies

"The only truth lies in learning to free ourselves
from the insane passion for the truth."

—UMBERTO ECO

The great golf teacher Harvey Penick said, "I don't wish to sound pretentious in any way, but I've always tried to teach by using stories or parables. I figure if it's good enough for the Bible, it's good enough for Harvey Penick."

Presumably Jesus taught in parables because stories are easier to remember, and if the story is a bit obscure, perhaps the hearer will ponder it and discover the hidden or more profound message. The new wine in old skins, new patch on old cloth parable, found in almost identical form in Matt. 9:17, Mark 2:21, and Luke 5:36, goes like this: "No man puts new wine in old bottles lest it burst them, and likewise, no person sews new cloth to patch an old garment, for it will tear it." Wine was made in those days in open containers for immediate fermentation after crushing and, after the most gaseous phase was done, into goat skins with the neck tied off for further storage and fermentation. The goat skins could stretch to accommodate fermentation, but if new wine was put in after they were fully stretched, they would burst. Likewise, an unshrunk cloth patch would pull at the edges of the old cloth and rip it. None of this was news to Jesus's audience, so what was his point?

The context was the Old Testament rules on fasting as well as the Pharisees' rules on most every other part of life. His message was new and wouldn't necessarily fit with the old. Because of tradition, inertia, and familiarity, old is what people usually want to keep doing. Luke's version says that no one drinking old wine desires new; old is better. Thus, Jesus is a revolutionary.

Gospel was what Jesus was selling as compared to the law of the Old Testament. Salvation by faith. A direct relationship with God. The old order found his message unsettling.

What did these parables mean to me sitting there in a balcony pew spacing out? I remember the wine part because the Presbyterians used grape juice for communion, and even at that age, I thought that was a candy-assed nod to the temperance crowd. Grape juice didn't even begin to remind me of the blood of Christ any more than the Wonder Bread did of the body. Needed some kick there.

If the message I should learn now is to be open to the new—new ideas, new learning, new opportunities—I heartily agree. If it is that the new must replace the old, I am less sanguine. My belief is that our functionality and our mental health depend on our understanding, to the greatest extent possible, everything that has happened to us over the course of our lifetimes and, historically, all human experience before us. The new may replace the old as in the Copernican revolution where Galileo and others challenged the Church's teaching that the sun revolved around the earth. Accommodations for what we know as truth have to be made based on new and reliable information. New truths are part of the joy and mystery of being human, but I confess to being a conservative in the sense that this should never be done lightly, never without compelling evidence and never for what Jefferson called "transient causes."

Death and life are central to Christian theology, but death was not a prominent part of my early years. All four of my grandparents were dead by the time I was three, so I knew none of them. My parents' friends were durable. When my classmate David Dunn died when I was in the eighth grade (he was playing in a ditch that collapsed), we didn't know what to do with it. As pallbearers, we stood around looking at each other, some crying and none of us knowing what this was all about.

A well-meaning minister told us that we would see him in heaven. Will his body be all crumpled up? What about all the mud? Will he always be thirteen years old? Lots of questions and not many useful answers. I cruised on through young adulthood pretty much untouched by death until college when a friend and fellow football player killed himself. President Kennedy was shot, and death came roaring in big time.

Everybody gets dead. I knew that, intellectually if not existentially, but now all those unthinking recitations in church came flowing back. "I believe in the resurrection of the body." It is in the Apostles' Creed, the Nicene Creed, and the Athanasian Creed. The second-string apostle Paul told the Corinthians that if the dead are not raised, "then Christ has not been raised. If Christ has not been raised, your faith is futile and you are still in your sins. Then those also who have fallen asleep in Christ have perished" (1 Cor. 15:13–18). Heavy. The entire Christian salvation depends on resurrection of the body, but if it isn't true, all dead believers will rot with the worms.

Paul wouldn't let up. To the Philippians he wrote that anyone who denies resurrection of the body is "the first born of Satan." Saint Augustine, in his earthy sort of way, wrote,

Perish the thought that the Creator is unable, for the raising of our bodies and restoring them to life, to recall all parts, which were consumed by beasts or by fire, or which disintegrated into dust or ashes, or were melted away into a fluid, or evaporated away into vapor.

—CITY OF GOD 22:20:1 (CE 419)

He was totally committed to reconstruction of the body.

I understand the fable of Genesis where God took clay, made a body, blew life into it, and made a soul and that a human is not whole without both, but at the risk of having Satan for a dad, I have never understood why the body has to go along to the hereafter.

Marcus Borg, the celebrated historical Jesus scholar, after a lifetime of searching, decided resurrection of the body didn't matter: He concluded that it was irrelevant whether or not the tomb was empty. Whether Easter involved something remarkable happening to the physical body of Jesus didn't affect the validity of the fundamental message.

This may be heresy to some, but I think shedding the two-thousand-year-old worldview and keeping the underlying wisdom makes a lot of sense.

CHAPTER 25

Firm Foundation

"Nationalism is the measles of mankind."
—ALBERT EINSTEIN

Not all of Jesus's parables are obscure. At the end of Matthew's retelling of the house built on a rock, he remarks: "The people were astonished at his doctrine, for he taught them as one having authority, and not as the scribes." This is more than just an opportunity to take an unscheduled swing at the Pharisees; it tells us that the people understood. This is one I do remember hearing in my youth. Harry Belafonte, who was all the rage then, sang a calypso song the words of which were, "House built on a firm foundation, it will stand, oh yes, story told through all creation, it will stand, oh yes." Chances are pretty good that the song got it into my head more effectively than the church sermon.

This is elemental stuff that everybody knows, right? Jesus says whosoever hears these sayings of mine and does them is like the man who built his house on a rock. Those who hear the word and ignore it are like the foolish man who built on sand and the rains and winds and waters swept it away and "great was the fall of it" (Matt. 7:24–27). Well, the developers of the celebrated Salishan Resort on the Oregon coast built a whole string of houses on the sand spit. Guess what happened.

The hymn's words are, "The church's one foundation is Jesus Christ our lord, He is the new creation of water and the word." These quotes of lyrics are coming out of my head, and if they are incorrect, that supports my point on how memory rearranges stuff. I also believe that unlike some art that is immutable, lyrics can for the most part be changed or even made up, like "Good King Wenceslas's car backed out on a piece of Stephen…"

Back to the firm foundation. It is good advice for almost everything. Want to learn a language? Conjugate verbs, drill on vocabulary, study sentence structure, listen to native speakers. Play basketball? Run and run and run some more. Dribble with your eyes closed, one hand and then the other. When the ball goes up, put that opposing player on your butt, and move him out. Footwork, footwork, footwork. Preparation, planning, and carry-through; that is the recipe for success.

Is my take on this parable the opposite of what Jesus sought? His rock is faith in his teachings. My takeaway is that success comes with hard work and preparation and faith in that training and in yourself. Oops.

I have been wondering whether we have switched from a work ethic to a play ethic. We care about sports scores. We care about Facebook and Snapchat and God knows what else is out there in social media. Our work brings dissatisfaction, few rewards, lots of cynicism, and insecurity. Machines and artificial intelligence will do much of the work humans do today. We have some serious societal reordering to do. Into this dissatisfaction vacuum has jumped all sorts of noxious rhetoric of blame, accusation, and insult. Certain religious leaders have seized this opportunity in a way that is most unholy. When the Pharisees were trying to trick him into making a political statement, Jesus demurred, saying to render unto Caesar that which is Caesar's and unto God that which is God's. Today's sellout of some Christian leaders to Trumpism is unbiblical and short-sighted and harms both politics and religion. The reason is stated clearly in the words of Reinhold Niebuhr from the last century: "Religion is so frequently a source of confusion in political life and so frequently dangerous to democracy precisely because it introduces absolutes into the realm of relative values."

I would think those of the Evangelical community who feature themselves as heaven-bound would be nervous. The Judeo-Christian message is clear: nobody sneaks into heaven. It is a believers-only club. Believers adhere to the word of God, not of politicians. Misdirection and constant testing are part of the journey. When the Prophet Isaiah is called before the throne of God, and there are six-winged seraphim, smoke, and live coals pressed against his lips, God says the people will hear and see but not understand. Isaiah is to "make the heart of this people fat, and make their ears heavy, and shut their eyes; lest they see with their eyes and hear with their ears, and understand with their heart, and convert and be healed" (Isa. 6:10). *Yo! Listen up.*

Three of the four Gospels Matt. 13:10–17, Mark 4:10–11, and Luke 8:10–11 carry the same fundamental message that the apostles get it, they understand and believe, but the great unwashed don't get to be spoon-fed. They get a diet of parables that they may or may not understand, believe, and embrace. Luke likens it to seeds (the word of God) being cast on rock where it springs up and withers, where it is choked by brambles and where initial believers sprout up but are picked off by the devil. Only seeds that fall on good soil and are cultivated get to heaven, and it takes patience.

Several centuries earlier, Plato did much the same in his dialogues, never revealing what Socrates really thought but expecting the students to puzzle it out for themselves. Misdirection is part of the mystery, and mystery is a major draw of religion. The great twentieth-century rabbinical scholar Abraham Heschel writes, "the beginning of our happiness lies in the understanding that life without wonder is not worth living."

Fine and dandy. How does this shake out with an eleven-year-old squirming around in the pew? It was part of what you had to endure before you could rip off the necktie, get on the bike, and disappear. The only moral lesson was patience, and there was precious little of that.

Patience is a major lesson of golf. Don't try to do too much with a single shot. Don't count your money while you're sittin' at the table (i.e., Gosh, I'm 3 under par after four holes. I'm going to win, and then the wheels come off).

Patience while you try to groove a new swing.

Patience while you heal from an injury.

Patience while you put the last bad shot out of your consciousness and plan the next.

Patience that your game plan (say, to hit for the middle of the green on every hole) is sound.

PART IV

Books as the Source of Ethics

CHAPTER 26

Saved by the Book

"When his book opens its mouth,
the author must shut his."

—FRIEDRICH NIETZSCHE

As challenging as I found reading to be (and it still is), I read a lot as a teenager. I remember books like *The Catcher in the Rye, Stranger in a Strange Land,* and the scary *Fahrenheit 451.* While I can't cite chapter and verse of any moral lessons, I knew books were necessary for any future I envisioned for myself. Books were how I was to learn; books would teach me about life. I valued books even more because I had to work so hard to conquer them.

Some fifty years later, I knew I was done with the practice of law when they took the books from the law library to the dump. A few of us, after anguished cries of protest, boxed up the remaining books and stored them in an airplane hangar, but that was a mere stay of execution. The space used for the law library in the Gallatin County, Montana, court house was given to the prosecutor's office, and all legal research thereafter was online. Parenthetically, all case law before 1991, which is how far back cases were electronically available at that time, was lost.

I believe a book, a real one that you can hold in your hand, turn the page, underline the profound passage, and admire on the shelf, has a soul. It can be caressed, reread, and pondered, and having the books I most adore around me is like being in a room full of my friends. Books have helped me unpack and understand my experiences. They have taught empathy and compassion.

We have spent millennia developing moral philosophy as a roadmap for how we interact as human beings. Our contemporary and historical authors are the repository of that wisdom. The problem is that invention is quicker than moral philosophy—it presents us with devices and options the ramifications of which we have not thought through, and this is particularly troubling since philosophy is the guide and technology the tool.

The law creating the National Endowment for the Arts and the National Endowment for the Humanities in the United States in 1965 stated the dilemma this way:

> *Democracy demands wisdom and vision in its citizens.*
> *It must therefore foster and support a form of education*
> *[and access] designed to make people of all backgrounds*
> *and wherever located masters of their technology and*
> *not its unthinking servant.*
>
> —20 USC 951(Sec.2(4)), 1965

Libraries, like museums, collect and preserve the best of what our civilizations have produced. They maintain that wisdom not to gather dust but to guide us, to inform us, to inspire us in the business of living our individual and collective lives. They are living institutions and are critical to our success as a people. Reading is cumulative, building on, modifying, or replacing what we have read before.

The library building itself makes a statement about what we value as a society: a communal place of learning and pleasure. The old Carnegie building in Medford was a style seen throughout the country with wide front steps, a high, imposing ceiling, and large open spaces. I would go there, or rather go along with my sister and brother, bewildered by the books and the wealth of opportunities they presented. I usually chose a book Dave had already read. At home, I labored over it. One thing caddying taught me was to persevere, to hang in there until I slogged all the way through it. Indeed, it is only recently (into my seventh decade) that I have been willing to abandon a book I find unrewarding before finishing it.

Libraries are a place of discovery. In the words of Marcel Proust, that voyage is not to find new landscapes but to find new eyes (although according to Mark Twain, most creativity is just undiscovered plagiarism).

Books and libraries celebrate the beauty of the language. Poetry is meant to be heard, to be shared, absorbed, and reflected by an audience. All books have the singular attribute of becoming real only when the writing bounces back from the reader's brain. Otherwise, it is just scratching on a page or screen. There is something communal and reassuring about reading together. We don't do enough of it. We did some family readings, but they were usually from the Bible. Mother, Good Book in hand, would declare that it was time for "family worship" to the groans from the rest of us, but those sessions reminded us that the written word had a vital role in reaffirming human dignity.

Sure, humans are cruel, selfish, dangerous, and petty, but we are also loving, generous, caring, and funny. The author lays bare all of these human characteristics, helps us connect to others, care for others, and afford all persons the dignity that is an essential part of our being. Authors teach us to care not for just humans but for animals and our environment, all of which are an essential part of keeping this small planet viable.

Since Medford did not have a real bookstore, the trips to the library gave me the keys to the kingdom—the treasures held by the library. At the library, I found adventure, wonder, escape, and, most importantly, the tools to do and be whatever I wanted. Education isn't about facts; it is about confidence in knowing how to get to the facts, where to find guidance, and what to trust. That is what reading lots of books teaches. Education is what remains when we have forgotten all that we have been taught.

CHAPTER 27

Believing Books

> "Being a writer is like having homework every
> night for the rest of your life."
>
> —LAWRENCE KASDAN

Writing is a gift, and unlike most Ponzi schemes, it increases in value the more it is shared, and it is legal. All writers are teachers, sharing what they know, think, or imagine with the rest of us. In my universe, the greatest honorific that can be bestowed on anyone is "teacher."

Outside the Kennedy Center in Washington, DC, is a small statue of Sancho Panza, the farmer turned squire and sidekick of Don Quixote in Cervantes' seventeenth-century novel—perhaps the best ever written. Panza follows his knight in bizarre quests and is a font of everyday wisdom. The caption underneath the statute says, "The enchanters may rob me of my good fortune but never of my spirit or my will." Each of us is potentially both a perpetrator and a victim in this brilliant glimpse of reality. We are the enchanters from whose lips drip political speak—the half-truths, hyperbole, self-deception, and subservience to the rich and powerful.

Each of us is the leader-hero who will not, no matter what happens, be deprived of that individual spirit that guides us to know what is right, who we are, and what we are willing to die for.

After I graduated from the life-observation school of caddying, I found multiple other sources of life instruction. I knew about sacred texts but also discovered great writers like Margaret Atwood, Toni Morrison, and Mark Twain. Nigger Jim in *Adventures of Huckleberry Finn* is an example of the truly moral man—the foil to Huck's moral meanderings. The book has been banned in the United States in nearly every generation, usually for a different reason. My take is that whenever a book is banned, it must be because it has something important to say.

Gustav Flaubert said, "We read in order to live." Stories are the portals where we store our experiences. We pull them down, retell them, modify them, and savor them because they connect us to ourselves and our place in this world.

Moral issues, at least the hard ones, are confusing. Books bring order to chaos and chaos to order; they comfort the afflicted and afflict the comfortable. Harriet Beecher Stowe on slavery, Rachael Carson on the environment, and Ralph Nader on auto safety are a few of a legion of examples of authors challenging the established order that I read in my teen years.

Books are subversive; that is why tyrants ban and burn them and why kids reading them sometimes make their parents nervous. One particularly memorable dinner conversation, more heated than most, was about a critique of our economic system. Michael Harington had just published *The Other America*, and we kids had read it at college and were going to take no prisoners. That maybe hit a little close to home for Dad since he was doing well thanks to that system. To his credit, he didn't try to shut us down; he just asked lawyerly questions and made us defend our passion.

Books celebrate ambiguity. The towering twentieth-century theologian Paul Tillich said, "The appreciation of the ambiguity of our greatest achievements as well as our deepest failures is a definite sign of moral maturity." In the world of justice, we deal in shades of gray. Separating out what is the business of the law and what of ethics is one of the major jobs and dilemmas of governments, societies, and neighborhoods. Good writers don't tell us what to do or what to think, but they pose the dilemmas and ask the questions so we know we are not alone in struggling with a hostile universe.

Authors don't get medals for bravery, but they should. It takes guts to lay it all out there, to bare one's soul, to risk the rejection, ridicule, and hatefulness that are the bitter gruel spit back by some readers (and even more by those who have not read the book but heard about it, probably from someone who hasn't read it either). We have much of which to be afraid, and we deny fear in our day-to-day lives, but what reader is afraid to turn the page? Our authors take on the fear for us and help us deal with it. As playwright Anton Chekov put it, "Man does not put on his best trousers when he goes out to fight for truth and justice." It is a necessary and messy business. One author of books on how to write fiction advises to write about that of which you are afraid. That, she says, is the best way to get to your authentic self and create characters who are real.

Poet Sam Hazo writes that all we keep of the truth is what we give away. If books do their job and we as readers do our job, something more has to come of it than just closing it and going to see what is in the fridge. Franz Kafka said, "I think we ought to read only books that bite and sting us. If [it] doesn't shake us awake like a blow on the skull, why bother." My definition of philosophy is thought translated into action. Thoughtful and considered action is the definition of life, and we are blessed to have books as our companions on the journey.

Books help us to ask the right questions. Forgive the oversimplification, but one way of looking at science is that it asks what the answer is, whereas the humanities ask what the question is. A recent article on Peter Thiel, founder of PayPal, described the millions of dollars he has contributed to scientists who are trying to do away with death. Without dwelling on the hubris involved in such an undertaking, suppose he were partially successful—extending the average life to 150 years—shouldn't someone be asking whether this a good idea? Some of the questions a reasonable humanist—an author—would ask are what happens to earth's resources, its capacity? What happens to the theology of religions that promise an afterlife? Would a country have to abide a cruel dictator for one hundred or more years? Should the individual desire to live forever trump the societal good of replenishing the gene pool? Should only people who can afford an extended life get one?

Are there any books about golf that I remember? No, but there are a lot of books about golf, one by John Feinstein using as a title Mark Twain's description *A Good Walk Spoiled*. Golf lends itself to writing because it is the individual's struggle against nature. It is like the Greek myth of Sisyphus. He is condemned by the gods to roll a stone almost to the top of a mountain only for it to roll down so he must continually start over. Albert Camus used this as a metaphor for the meaning-lessness of life, for its absurdity. He argued that humankind can rebel by embracing the hopelessness, learning to enjoy it, and taking our identity from it. Golf, anyone?

CHAPTER 28

Book Power

"There are some ideas so wrong that only a very intelligent person could believe them."

—George Orwell

I have heard it plenty of times in court, "That is an argument that could fool only a lawyer." Unfortunately, more than a few of such arguments are successful in the sense that they carry the day and win the case. Sometimes such numbskull ideas are unmasked by appellate courts, and sometimes more lawyers are fooled at the appellate level. We can think ourselves stupid.

To what extent are books culpable in misleading us? They are not as bad as what is on the web, which is like saying, "Well, he is not as bad as Hitler." Unlike the web, books are printed (except for the ones that are on the web) and are therefore a permanent iteration meant to hang around as long as some person or library retains a copy. They state their position, and it is immutable until the next edition comes out, which, in the case of most books, is never. The authors are not slinging some nonsense out there in the electronic biosphere; they are writing it down on paper and challenging us to believe or challenge back.

Traditional wisdom holds that books, particularly fiction, teach us empathy by our identification with the characters and their struggles and moral dilemmas. They teach about injustice, about suffering, about wars—not glorious wars but wars with mud, death, cold, disease, cruelty, and waste. They teach that the brave and the just may perish, and the cowards and scoundrels survive. They teach that wars beget wars.

Is reading moral? It has the power to mold moral views, but what if that is all it does? Suppose, in different generations with different moral issues, a person read Harriet Beecher Stowe's *Uncle Tom's Cabin*, Rachel Carson's *Silent Spring*, and Ralph Nader's *Unsafe at Any Speed* and, with a yawn and a stretch, wondered what was for lunch? Can we blame the book for failing to provoke moral action? I think not, but if reading the book gives the reader permission to say, in effect, "I know about this issue now and am a better person for it, and that is all I have to do," the result is no result. A waste.

I knew of a person in Livingston, Montana, who saw *Schindler's List*, the movie based on *Schindler's Ark* by Thomas Keneally, and identified with the Nazis. He suggested to his employer that the Jews ought to be stacked up like cordwood and burned. The author cannot be blamed for human stupidity and human evil.

Books can overwhelm us. Early in my career, I practiced with a lawyer, a brilliant mind, who was a hopeless lawyer because he could not stop researching a $1,000 issue until he had logged $5,000 worth of time. There was surely one more case that would be on point. The majesty of the law rendered him ineffectual.

I am revealing my prejudice for action, because I believe morality is considered ideas put into action. A criticism of philosophers and many academics is that they have become so specialized, so knowledgeable in a narrow area, that their world of minutia renders them irrelevant. An example from a few years back is when I was a keynote speaker in a meeting of architects, and I suggested in my talk that they could be leaders with artistic solutions to urban problems. The person putting together the book on the symposium informed me that my talk was not suitable for inclusion because it had nary a footnote, and the others had spent five or six years researching their topics. Okay, the speech got a standing ovation, but hey, if the criteria is how arcane it is, action is unlikely to follow.

I am not suggesting that scholarship is irrelevant. On the contrary, it is the lifeblood of learning. My point is that learning must result in action if moral issues are at stake.

PART V

Eighteen Holes of Ethical Musings

THE FIRST HOLE

Playing with Fire

"Happiness is the absence of striving for happiness."
—CHUANG TZU

amp White was a military training base during World
War II out in the sagebrush and foxtails of the prairie
northeast of Medford. Glenn Jackson was a mover
and shaker temporarily tormenting the Germans during the
war, best known for creating double-decker Quonset huts for
office space in England and having his men pitch the Italians'
typewriters out the windows when the GIs needed space in
a hurry after the war moved there. Returning from the war,
Colonel Jackson acquired Camp White (don't ask), renamed
it White City, and turned it into an industrial park where
sawmills transformed one hundred railroad carloads of logs
into boards each day. This is the same Glenn Jackson who
owned the golf course.

There was nothing white about White City. It was brown
and dusty with flecks of sawdust flying around. Summer
temperatures there reached 110 degrees. Dave and I were
employed as maintenance men thanks to Dad's connection

with Col. Jackson, for whom he did legal work. Under the supervision of Jerry Fletcher, who reminded us of Doberman on the *Sgt. Bilko* television show, our job was to pick up scrap lumber wherever we found it (and it was everywhere), throw it into our '47 Dodge dump truck, drive to the dump, and discharge it—hopefully onto a burning pile so we wouldn't have to light it. The trick was to dump it so it would burn but not back so far into the pile that the truck would burn too. One of our fellow dumpers waited a little too long to pull out and toasted his truck.

Fire was a big part of White City. The dump was always burning, and wigwam burners, those giant, thimble-shaped domes with wire mesh at the top, took care of most of the wood waste. This was before lumber mills became more efficient in using most of the tree and long before anyone gave a rat's ass about pollution. I remember several sawmill fires along with assorted brush and building fires, only one of which I was personally responsible for (more on that in a minute).

Our foreman, Jerry, was full of aphorisms: "We don't want the boss to think we are just puttin' in our time and that's all," "It's like milkin' a cow with boxing gloves on," "You can't swat a fly with a tennis racket." I pitched a sticker over the truck one morning and hit him in the back of the head. I was not his favorite worker for a week or so, but he got over it and was good humored, kind to us, and entertaining. He said we did main-tain-ence. We were main-tain-ence engineers. I adored Jerry.

One day, my job was to do some on-purpose burning in a weed field on the Medford side of White City. This was to be a fire line to protect the buildings to the North. I found, with my flat-bladed shovel, that once the fire got going, I could flip up some of the ground sawdust, and it would go "poof" like a sparkler. "Hey Dave, look at this!" Poof, and the whole field is on fire.

I was lucky. The wind was from the North, and the fire department showed up and corralled it. No one asked how the fire got started.

Perhaps because I was the go-to fire guy, I was given a job the next year to burn some tree parts that had been uprooted and bulldozed into piles in the course of clearing ground for more construction. I was given a backpack sprayer full of gasoline and instructed to saturate the piles and light them. That didn't work very well, because the gas would whoosh up, sending me jumping back, but after the whoosh, not much happened. I found that if I got the fire going and squirted gas onto it from my backpack sprayer, the damn things would burn. How I didn't turn into a potato chip, I do not know. It is a wonder that any of us survive to adulthood, but this is a chapter in my youth that makes me shiver every time I think of it.

Putting the two fire stories together, should I have confessed that I started the field fire? Would there have been some benefit in doing so, and if so, to whom?

If the fire had zipped right back up my gas line and burned me to a crisp, who would be to blame? Me, of course, because I was being a juvenile dumbshit. My employer for not instructing me, not supervising me, and choosing that method of burning in the first place. People do dumb things. Part of the business of morals is to forgive and part is to instruct. Obviously, I didn't learn much about the propensity of fire to take off from my first adventure. Fire is dangerous, and turning a kid loose with a gas sprayer, which shouldn't have been used for that purpose in the first place, and leaving me unsupervised was criminally negligent.

The moral query here is to what extent we are our brother's keeper? The law keeps us from intentionally putting others in harm's way by requiring handrails, crosswalks, and the like. Even if there were no law preventing a weed sprayer from being used as a flamethrower, was there some moral obligation for not putting me in danger? We think about these issues—about taking care of each other and preventing harm—to prevent tragedies. The moral finger shaking is less useful than moral instruction that helps us proactively to prevent harm.

THE SECOND HOLE

Teaching

"I have never let my schooling interfere
with my education."

—MARK TWAIN

Paul Evanson was a football player, a history teacher,
and the line coach of the Medford High School Black
Tornado. We started the dreaded two-a-day practices in
September when it was reliably one hundred-plus degrees in the
Rogue Valley. Morning practice was easier—not so hot and not
so sore, and we could stop for a quart of A&W root beer after.
Afternoons were in the heat of the day, and about four days in, I
asked him to excuse me while I ran to the sidelines to throw up.
"Need a replacement for a yorker," I heard him say.

He had played in college—for Oregon State, I think—and
severed the muscle on his right bicep during a game. They
slapped some tape on it, and he played the rest of the game. Arm
never was the same. He was a big, bald guy and smart. Many
coaches taught history in those days as if history didn't matter
much and anyone could spew off a bunch of dates. He was a great
guy; a mentor, not a role model. Someone worth listening to.

One time at practice, he was explaining some footwork mistake I had made, and I said, "You're right." He turned to another coach and said, "John says I'm right. Wadda ya think of that? Ain't that great?"

He was also the golf coach. He had all of the swing flaws that those coming late in life to the game adopt: slow, awkward backswing as if to sneak up on the ball and then a lunge to try to get it before it escaped. Coaching high school golf consisted of showing up at the country club, playing with one or more of the team members (we never practiced as in putting or hitting balls—we just played), and driving us to our matches in his unadorned, green '55 Chevy four door. The Chevy had bench seats that could hold five golfers and Paul. This was before the days of seatbelts, so we piled in and took off. Paul would get tired of driving after a while and say, "You drive, John," which I did. I was sixteen or seventeen. Mike Monroe, a year younger and about two decades smarter in the ways of the world, constantly reminded Paul that he (Mike) had brought his license, but he never got to drive. I shudder to think, in today's litigious world, what would have happened had I stacked us all up.

We would check into some decrepit fleabag hotel, say in Marshfield. Dark halls and unlocked adjoining room doors. Mike decided he would take a bath in the room next door. Paul found out and said, "If the rooms we get you aren't good enough..." and we all felt ashamed. Not much shame attached to stealing, however. There seemed to be a moral holiday when teams travelled, and this was true in my experience with all sports. Tony came back with a necktie—said it folded up in his hand and leapt into his pocket. Cuff links were a favored item to be purloined. On the road and away from our parents the normal rules were suspended.

I came late to golf practice one day because I had been necking with my girlfriend in her car. All the others were already playing, so it was Paul and me. He gave me a funny look but only said, "Let's go." We played nine, and in the locker room afterward, I realized I had lipstick all over my face. That was one of many episodes that endeared him to me, but I never asked him about it when I visited him in his declining years.

I have always revered and, in a lot of ways, envied career teachers. They put up with wheelbarrow loads of crap from multiple directions: big time from the kids and from parents, administrators, school boards, taxpayers. It is hard work, one of the most demanding professions I know. Keeping fresh and motivated when the pay is so low and the rewards so ephemeral takes a real love of kids and learning. Teachers have told me that they hope, over the course of a career, they have touched—really made a difference—in the lives of a dozen students.

Education is critical to the survival of a democracy. The First Amendment protects speech and the press, because we need accurate information and the ability to parse that information and draw out the truth to guide our government in a system where the people own it. When I was in high school, almost all of the teachers had summer jobs because the pay was so meager. One day, Dave and I arrived at a lumberyard to pick up some materials we needed to do our main-tain-ence, and there was Dave's math teacher, waiting on us.

It is a democracy on its way to oblivion that does not pay attention to education.

Workers

> "If you don't have a seat at the table,
> you are probably on the menu."
>
> —Anonymous

His name was Harry Pitts. Really. I worked with him at the concrete pipe plant in Central Point one summer along with a guy named Hall and a young guy whose name was also John—the one who said with a straight face, "I wish my wife had been a fuckin' virgin." They made concrete pipe from six-inch drain tile to mammoth culvert size. My job was to paint the lip of the big pipes with cement, move stuff around, make drain tile, drive truck, clean up, and do whatever needed doing.

I was a college kid and therefore suspect. I noticed that Harry had sardines in his lunch as I sat with my fellow workers, trying to be quiet and listen. I asked Mom to put some sardines in my lunch, and Harry said, "Ya got fish, John." I knew that on some level, I had been accepted. I worked hard, did everything asked. I learned the dignity of men (no women did this work then) who worked physically hard for a living.[3] Harry had a 1932 Dodge Coupe that I coveted. He took me for a ride, showed me how to adjust the spark on the center of the steering column, poured on the gas, and scared the shit out of me. I was thereafter perfectly happy with my '51 Ford. It had brakes.

As far as I could tell, every man at the pipe plant lived from paycheck to paycheck, and all of them, because it was a union shop, had to belong to the teamsters. They warned me that the union steward would be by to sign me up. What benefit would I get as a summer employee? They said they would keep a lookout and tip me off when he showed up so I could go hide. I successfully dodged around the pipe yard the first couple of times, but the third time, there were two of them, and they cornered me. "What do I get out of joining?" They didn't try to justify it; they just said, "We will shut down the pipe plant if you don't." I paid my dues, got my teamsters card, and felt kind of proud of it.

The company ran a rock crushing operation near Prospect on the road toward Crater Lake. I was dispatched—I had a commercial driver's license, fitting for a card-carrying teamster—in an old flatbed with many tired but seemingly functional parts to haul back a piece of a rock crusher that needed repair. I got there. A crane loaded an impossibly large and heavy piece of metal, and the foreman said, "Take it slow, John." Yeah, 'cause if I hit the brakes and they worked, this monster would slide right through the headache rack and

---

3   Herman Melville (wrote *Moby Dick*) had a different take: "They talk of the dignity of work. Bosh. The dignity is in the leisure." But hey, this is the guy who wrote the book where Ahab chases the whale, and the whale sinks his ship.

crush me like a bug. I wondered if the teamster membership entitled me to life insurance. Slow is how I took it.

Work is dangerous. People get hurt, and when they are hurt, they can't work. The law says that workers can't sue their employer for an on-the-job injury except in limited circumstances. In exchange for this legal disability, there is a system of scheduled compensation to which the worker is entitled without showing culpability on the part of the employer or freedom from negligence on the part of the employee. It is called Worker's Compensation, and employers are taxed for this benefit based on safety ratings, inherent dangers of the job, and various other rating mumbo jumbo.

From a worker's point of view, the payments are hardly compensatory. How many dollars is the loss of an arm worth? Perfect justice would restore the use of the arm, but perfect justice is not available for humankind, so money is the substitute. The big debate society is having with itself now is a moral one: To what extent is the government obligated to provide a safety net for people who cannot care for themselves? This includes not just injured workers but the mentally ill, the poor, the homeless, the food insecure, the medically needy. The bogeyman word for such state-supported care is socialism. We have had socialized medicine in the form of Medicare and Medicaid since 1965, but those don't seem to count in the realm of those who believe that once the word socialism is uttered, whatever follows is a bad idea.

We need to have the moral debate before the political one. As citizens of the richest country in the history of the world, is it our obligation to provide for our fellow citizens? If the answer is yes, the next moral/political step is to decide who is included and if any are excluded. The third step is to find the political solution based on a moral consensus. We don't do things that way. Politics is the first resort for almost everything, and the moral questions get squished beneath the dumpster loads of political garbage spewing from all corners of our everyday world.

THE FOURTH HOLE

Bad Sports

"If there is one thing that golf demands
above all else, it is honesty."

—JACK NICKLAUS

Poor sportsmanship breaks out all the time in golf, much of it nasty. The most egregious example I experienced was in the high school state championships where we were playing at Glendoveer in Portland. The course was new to me, and we hadn't arrived in time for a practice round, so I asked one of my playing partners—a competitor from another school—where one should hit his drive on a downhill par 5. He said, "Hit it along that tree line to the right," which, amazingly, I did. He said, "Oh, that is out of bounds over there." I couldn't believe it. We finished the round, and I found my teammates Tom Hamlin and Tony Monroe sitting at the bar having a beer. I was surprised since you couldn't legally drink unless you were twenty-one. I told them what had happened, and they were willing to beat the crap out of the kid, at least theoretically, but wanted to finish their beers first.

Remember, golf claims a conceited righteousness in that you are expected to call penalties on yourself. While some of these rules have recently changed, for eons, if you replace your ball after marking it and it rolls: penalty. If you discover you have more than fourteen clubs in the bag: penalty. If you are addressing the ball and it moves more than a quarter turn: penalty. If your wedge hits the ball in flight (a double hit): penalty. Most embarrassing of all, if you swing at it and miss (a whiff), it costs one stroke unless you swing and miss again—strike 2. If no one is looking, how many of these penalties are actually called? In friendly golf, does it matter? In tournament golf, it can cost a lot of money.

One golfer I knew of was called even-tempered by his friends: mad all the time. Tommy Bolt, a celebrated pro of my youth, was known for his temper. He always threw the club forward so he wouldn't have to walk back for it. Bobby Rasmussen, older than me by a lot, was said to have scars on his knees from the club shafts he had broken over them. I have seen marks in the green where players buried their putter heads upon missing a short one. I saw Wayne Sabin baseball swing an 8-iron through a laurel hedge when he knew he was losing the match. I have seen players improve their lies on the fairway when summer rules are in effect and move the ball with the club head for a better lie in the rough. I have seen players step behind the ball in the rough for a better lie and twist branches out of the way. I have been told to write scores on the card that were one and sometimes two strokes light. I've seen a player, disgusted with his performance, walk off the green to the next hole without waiting for his playing partner to hole out. Beyond rude.

There was a guy named Harry, a total douchebag who, after he was up several holes on my master in match play, took out his pocket watch, put it down on the tee box with some grass on top, and hit his drive off it. Left us speechless. Rumor had it that Harry had been a pro but somehow regained his amateur status—like getting revirginized.

A doctor who was accustomed to having his orders obeyed was charged with and convicted of mayhem for strangling a goose that insisted in squawking and pooping on the green. Geese used to fly south for the winter, but now many choose to hang around northern climes, and apparently the healer thought this one did not deserve his professional care. He was having a bad day; the goose, a worse one.

All this is not without humor. "What would you have to shoot tomorrow to win your match? My opponent." "Why are you playing with a new putter? Because my old one didn't float." Will Rogers said, "Only the income tax has made more liars out of the American people than golf." P. G. Wodehouse: "A woman is just a woman, but a hefty drive is a slosh."

Galleries are not immune from poor sportsmanship such as yelling "you da man" in the player's backswing, crowding into the path the ball will take out of the woods, clicking cameras, shouting racial epithets. While the rules of the game itself are different from the rules of society, the rules of spectatorship should be much the same. College basketball games at most schools have a video of a student athlete advising that good sportsmanship is a team value and that heckling players, coaches, or officials is disrespectful. Schools will eject unruly fans from the game and investigate instances of racial slurs, all of which is right and good. A standing boo for a bad call seems still to be within the bounds of acceptable behavior.

THE FIFTH HOLE

Golf Here and There

"The secret of life is honesty and fair dealing.
If you can fake that, you've got it made."

—GROUCHO MARX

Kirk West was a big, beefy bald guy—God's guy, actually. He had served as a missionary in China until Mao rolled in, and he came to serve the First Presbyterian Church in Medford just as I was coming into what some might call my formative years. He wasn't a great preacher. Time and again he would urge that Christ have a seat at the table in "that business deal," but most of the congregants seemed pretty facile in separating what happened on Sunday morning from the rest of the week.

He was a great guy—a guy's guy—a valuable and positive force for good. To me, he was a mentor and, in a lot of ways, a role model. In golf, he was a duffer: enthusiastic and predictably lousy. In town he was called Doctor West (okay, it was an honorary doctorate, but who is to quibble). Others called him pastor. I don't remember what I called him.

In the summer of 1965 when I was in graduate school, Kirk led a group of Presbyterian clergy and laity on a trip to the Far East to study higher education and rapid social change. He asked me to go along to "represent youth," which I took to be as much of a qualification as the ability to give a urine sample, but I wanted to go—to learn.

Somewhere in Taiwan or maybe Bangkok, we were staying in a hotel, and a stripper was in the lounge whose performance, not surprisingly, consisted of taking off her clothes. Ray Heysell, the other representative of youth, and I were having a beer and enjoying the pleasures of the flesh when Pastor West/Doctor Kirk came in and sat down at our table. Ray tried to un-order the beer and chaser he had requested, but since the evidence of what we had consumed was already on the table…eek. Pastor West/Doctor Kirk began chatting as if we were in the fireside room of the church while above us on the stage, Miss Candy Barr was flinging off her clothes and shaking her booty. Later in the trip, it became clear that most of the male and several of the female members of our entourage had sampled the charms of Candy Barr. I suppose there was a rapid social change message there. I had never thought of this, but his name was West, and he was a minister: West-minister. Someone should name a cathedral after him.

Because he was an enthusiastic golfer and a persuasive guy, Pastor West/Doctor Kirk talked us onto Wack Wack in the Philippines, saying that he had two top-flight young golfers with him. That attracted a crowd around the first tee. Pastor West/Doctor Kirk chunked a huge divot that went farther than his ball. Ray sliced, I hooked, and the crowd disappeared. While GIs were still fondly prized in the Philippines, we went a long way toward destroying any notion of American prowess.

Several years later, again in the Far East but this time with the US Navy, my ship pulled into the harbor in Singapore, and the injection temperature (that is the water coming into our condensers from the sea) was 97 degrees Fahrenheit. That is, an ocean as warm as a bath. Outside, the regular air was hot, sticky, and oppressive. Golf was definitely in order because the alternative was to stay on the ship and swelter. Our caddies were giggly young women in robin's egg-blue hard hats. I didn't believe her on the second hole when she handed me a 6-iron, so I hit a 9 and came up thirty yards short. We had leather grips on the clubs in those days, and one had to hold a towel, wipe hands, grip, and hit—no practice swing, or the club would squirt out of your hands on your next backswing.

Rab Minto, the chaplain of Memorial Church at Stanford when I was there, told of playing in India where if your ball went into the rough, you took a club, and if the cobra raised itself, you kept your eye on the target and swung as if your life depended on it. Here I played pretty well, and my caddie said, "Hey, MacKenzo, when you come back?" I think she thought I looked like Kennedy, and like Jack, I was not likely to come back.

In the Philippines, my caddie swung my clubs, helped himself to a cigar in my bag, and when he got tipped less than his fellow caddie, protested, "But I could have stolen your watch." For reasons unknown to me, I played some of my best golf docking in a port, walking onto a course I had never seen, and swinging away.

As a volunteer billet on the ship, I was athletics officer. There was method in my madness, since after I had organized various picnics and games for the crew, I made my case to the executive officer that I and two others should represent the ship in the all-Navy golf tournament in Japan. Problem was we were off the coast of Vietnam. Problem solved. The five-inch guns stopped shooting, Klingaman, Schneider, and I, with clubs over our shoulders, climbed into the admiral's helo and lifted off to Vung Tau. The admiral's plane flew us to Saigon where we caught a MATS flight to Atsugi in Japan. War is hell.

We all played badly at Atsugi but had fun, snuck our wives into the bachelor officers' quarters, and pretended we were civilians. The massage I had where the Japanese woman walks on your back left me with a two-week charley horse in my left calf.

I have belonged to two Springhill Country Clubs, have lived in a community named Springhill, grew up on Spring Street, and have quaffed spring water. The one in Bozeman had lots of water, and in the winter, when the course was not completely covered with snow, there would be half a dozen balls on the pond ice. I played, in separate pairings, with two of the world's most famous penguin researchers and a former Secret Serviceman. A client told me that a certain well-known man featured himself irresistible to whatever women were present after a second glass of wine. That evidence remains hearsay, but the social interactions of country clubs doesn't seem to have changed much in the sixty-five years since I was a caddie.

THE SIXTH HOLE

Getting Out of It

"There is no comfort zone in golf."

—TIGER WOODS

"Almost anything is easier to get into than out of." It is a saying, not a parable. It is sometimes known as Agnes Allen's Law, although I have no idea of who Agnes Allen is. Here are some examples.

Sand traps. Most golfers can't play sand for beans. Part of the reason is that they never practice from the sand. Part is that many club traps have shit for sand (pro tournaments have silicon sand that is precisely milled, and they know exactly how to hit, so sand is often easier than a chip from the grass). Sand traps in the fairway are distance killers. Pot bunkers on English links courses are so deep and difficult that the only escape may be back up the fairway, away from the green. The coolest sand I know is the coal-black sand of The Old Works course in Anaconda, Montana. It is built on the Superfund site of an old copper mine. The black sand is from copper tailings and has been milled to PGA specifications. It is almost a pleasure to be in. Almost.

Wars. During my lifetime, there has been a war in which the United States has had some involvement an average of every six years. I fought in Vietnam, the war where our strategy was to send our patrols out to get ambushed so artillery and air strikes could hammer the hidden enemy. Our troops as cannon fodder; some strategy. We didn't get out of it, we just left. After the attacks of September 11, we attacked Afghanistan, notwithstanding that nineteen of the twenty-one hijackers came from Saudi Arabia, which both then and now we say is our ally. History was no teacher for us either in Vietnam, where the French got whacked at Dien Bien Phu by Ho Chi Minh's siege, or in Afghanistan where the Soviets invaded, got roughed up, and after ten years, left. We have been fighting there for seventeen years, and there is no end and no victory in sight.

Marriage. Saying "I do" is a lot easier than arguing over who gets the dishes during splitsville. Kids are the real losers when they become pawns in the fight between two people who pledged to love each other and couldn't do it.

Jail. I don't think anyone sets out with the goal of being incarcerated. Maybe they were drunk, young, stupid. Probably all three, but once you are in the slam, a world of opportunities from voting to getting a job is closed to you. What you learn in jail is how to become a "better" criminal, the lessons being taught by those who weren't swift enough to avoid being caught.

Fights. I don't mean just fisticuffs but relationship-destroying arguments caused by temper tantrums, lack of self-control, or plain bad judgment. It is easier to call someone a fool than to produce responses that ask questions. Example: A guy in a restaurant is talking loudly, saying that all Democrats want to let a bunch of no-good Mexican criminals into the country. You could: a) ignore him; b) go stand over his table and tell him he is a nincompoop; or c) say, "I couldn't help but overhear your comment, and I wonder if you could help me understand why the Democrats would want that." Chances are no one will be persuaded by whatever dialogue follows, but at least you can take solace in knowing that you stood up for what you believed. The golf analogy is tempo—not escalating too soon, keeping things smooth, even, and under control, letting the club do the work in its proper measure.

Lies. My theory is that unless you are a pathological liar where you can't tell truth from falsehood or you don't care, most lies come from lack of mental preparation. You are surprised by a question and think the truth will hurt you, so you make up something and then have to keep prevaricating, each time getting in deeper and deeper. I know of one tragic case where a lawyer lied under oath, went back after lunch break and recanted, and still was convicted of perjury and sent to prison. It doesn't take much to ruin a reputation, or at least that used to be true when a reputation for truthfulness was the coin of the realm.

One thing I did manage to get out of was my Christian faith. It started, of all places, at Union Seminary in New York, where the beliefs I had accepted because they were my parents' could not withstand the challenge of rigorous study. I continued to go to church out of a sense of duty, took the kids to Sunday school, and then stopped. Not until after Mother died did I say publicly that I was not a believer.

The concept of God is a mystery. I can buy that, embrace that. Beyond such an appreciation, I believe we have no capacity to know the mind of God. Those who claim to know

God's will in any given earthly situation are, in my view, not worthy of belief. An agnostic is defined as one who believes that the existence, will, or capacity of God is unknowable. I am squarely in that camp. If we as humans could know the mind of the creator, we would not be human, and she would not be God.

I knew of a movement—perhaps better described as a couple of guys—who concocted a god named Bob whose sole function was to cut us some slack. They were having fun, but the idea is worthy. For our own mental health, we need to be able to forgive ourselves. We are imperfect beings, and we will fail. Even when we succeed, we could have done better. We wallow in regrets, in self-loathing, in hot-blooded frustration.

We can learn to be our own best friend. We can be nonjudgmental of failures that matter less and loving critics of those that are crucial, and we can teach ourselves the difference. A self-help book I didn't read but like the title of is *Don't Sweat the Small Stuff and It's All Small Stuff.*

How, you might ask? One way is by preparation and practice. A wizened trial lawyer responded to my question of how he took the pressure by saying, "I didn't make the law, and I didn't make the facts, and it's not my money." If I am fully prepared for a trial and lose, I am not going to like it, but do I need to put on sackcloth and ashes?

I can build confidence in myself. Sure, others are smart, perhaps smarter, but I can take stock of my abilities and maximize them by the profession I choose, the games I play, and those I finesse. I can learn from my mistakes, have a plan, be flexible. I can cultivate personal behavior that confers dignity on those who are my coworkers and my competitors. Even in the most tense, competitive situations I have encountered, a feeling that we are all in it together makes it infinitely more tolerable.

You can take your big white dog to work. Vladimir was a male Samoyed and the sweetest-dispositioned dog I have ever had. He went to the office with me on the day of a particularly difficult mediation, a case I thought would never settle. When the mediator got up to take the opposition to another room to confer, Vladimir got up, went with them, and stayed with them throughout the day. Each time we split up to confer, he went with them. He didn't ask for part of my fee when we settled, but he deserved it.

Reflecting on Wee-Wee

"God is the imagination."

—Wallace Stevens

P hilosophers have long debated the issue of free will.
Can we, by intellect and determination, direct our
actions and our lives, or are we fooling ourselves in a
universe where what we do, no matter how much we think we
are in control, is predetermined? Libertarians tend to believe
that free will is inconsistent with determinism; it has to be
one or the other. Others are more nuanced.

Two examples of determinism from different times and
perspectives are Sophocles' play *Oedipus Rex*, where Oedipus
is predetermined to kill his father and marry his mother no
matter how he tries to avoid it, and John Calvin's theory of
Christian predestination: at the apocalypse, some go up, and
some go down.

On the other side of the ledger, the free will side, are
some neuroscientists, physicists (not all of them in either
case), and Kant with his theory of deontology. Kant argues
that we act out of duty, and the intention of the action, not

its outcome, determines whether an action is moral. His categorical imperative, oversimplified, holds that one should act only in a way that would apply to everyone. Instead of looking at the front end of an action, philosopher Jeremy Bentham concentrated on the result—the greatest good for the greatest number: utilitarianism. Remember the ten-year-old boy who said he would take a bullet for his classmates in chapter 16? He is a utilitarian. Better one dead than twenty-three. What philosophers "discover" about humankind may be buried deep within us.

Sigmund Freud postulated that the human mind is made up of three parts: the ego, the id, and the superego. The ego is our conscious self. The id is our animal self, operating beneath our conscious level and urging us to animal actions such as aggression, sex, and satisfying desires. The superego is our conscience, again operating below the level of consciousness and often doing battle with the id to urge us to do the right thing.

Here is an embarrassing example from my youth. Mother was always late, so waiting for her was an expected part of my growing up. There we were, Dave and I, with baseball gloves and bulging bladders in the hot sun next to the old wooden baseball stadium. He was eight and I was six but about the same size because I was "big for my age." I said, "I can't hold it any longer" and just let go and peed my pants. Dave was horrified. "Why'd you do that?" Why indeed? I could have peed on the ground; nobody would have cared. Why'd I do that?

Humiliating. I was standing there watching my khakis turn dark with the hot wee-wee filling my tennies. Mother drove up, Dave whined, "Johnny wet his pants" and sat as far on the other side of the back seat as he could. I had a choice, didn't I? Why did I mess myself? Why did I feel so ashamed? Who was calling the shots in my young life?

Big old Lincoln. Had a smiley chrome grill like a shark with orthodonture and all the new stuff: push-button doors and electric windows. It was used. Otto never bought anything new—Second-Hand Otto, we called him—but this baby had twelve cylinders, a fastback, and nice gray upholstery that was getting soaked with my quickly cooling urine that started to smell like old sweat socks.

I don't remember what mother said. I didn't get scolded. She knew I felt terrible. Nobody else was involved in the sense that peeing my pants didn't harm anyone, but shame was mine. Ashamed for my lack of self-control. Guilt is supposed to be the internally generated emotion and shame the one that is imposed from the outside by society. I shamed myself.

What does this have to do with golf anyway? One of golf's virtues is that there is time for reflection while the game is going on. Walking between shots gives the opportunity to plan the next shot and put the last disastrous swing out of your mind, to gain perspective. Few action sports allow this luxury, but life requires it. If morality is about anything, it is evaluating our actions, our challenges, and making decisions based on that analysis.

I am in the free will camp: ethics is for action. If there is some predetermined cosmic hand pulling the strings, I can't know it, do anything about it, or change it, so I might as well act as if I am the master of my fate and the captain of my soul.

Which brings me, in this muddled musing, to the issues of conformity and individuality. Much of the moral instruction I remember as a youth was to be nice, respectful, polite, to fit in and go along. Restrain your anger, don't make a scene, don't rock the boat. These are all necessary to some extent for society to function. The danger is substituting conformity for moral maturity.

We should be angry and act on that anger when our education system sucks, homeless and food-insecure people are freezing on the streets, and our leaders are morons. We are taught from childhood that anger is bad—one of the seven deadly sins. Being nice all the time can be as morally lax as being an asshole. We should take it upon ourselves to find accurate information rather than swallowing whole the invective and half-truths that spew at us electronically from all sides of the political spectrum.

We are hardwired to demand justice and fairness, and yet we are blinded to these rights for those outside the clan. The clan can be the nation, the political party, the corporation, the neighborhood, or the family. Each of us must apply our individual morality in judgment of the actions of clans and nations—no easy task since our self-image is tied to that of the clan.

I am a senior fellow of the American Leadership Forum, a program dedicated to the proposition that leadership can be taught and that a network of leaders from diverse endeavors can buttress society. In our training, we learn that collective/ collaborative leadership decisions are superior to individual ones. I don't doubt that that is generally true but not always. People of goodwill have different opinions and beliefs. They gather information differently. Politeness often causes us to defer. Consensus can produce a bleached and sexless product in a situation calling for bold action. Requiring consensus can lead to paralysis. Sometimes somebody has to decide.

There is a difference between decency and morality. When I was chairman of the National Endowment for the Arts from

1989 to 1992, Senator Jesse Helms inserted language into our legislation that required that we "take into consideration general standards of decency" in giving our grants. In his universe, that meant don't give any awards to artists who are homosexuals. We finessed the language by acknowledging that our panelists who recommended the grant awardees represented decency in and of themselves.

Decency can mean that the person is considered upright by a society that is itself immoral. Take the Jim Crow South. Isabel Wilkerson's brilliant and deeply disturbing book *The Warmth of Other Suns* recounts the systemic indignities to which blacks were subjugated from lynchings, separate drinking fountains, and economic extortion to not being allowed to pass a white driver no matter how slowly they were going. Jim Crow existed from shortly after the Civil War, when reconstruction proved ineffectual, to the 1970s and maybe beyond. Throughout that time there were lots of "decent" people living with and tolerating, if not actively promoting, a highly immoral society. At a minimum, it brings into question whether patience is a virtue or a vice, a point Martin Luther King, Jr. makes in his "Letter from Birmingham Jail."

It also raises the question about how much of morality is dependent on time and place. Can we backdate our present moral beliefs to condemn a prior time? Is broom cleaning the past different from learning from history? Does it matter what is/was possible? Where does one get the moral courage to buck the headwind of a whole society's beliefs?

Morality, or at least what governments cloak themselves with to appear legitimate, changes depending on who has power. Recently, the majority leader of the Senate refused a hearing to one president's Supreme Court nominee, but when the president changed and a new nominee appeared, he talked of the senate's solemn duty to advise and consent with a straight face. Compare Vladimir Lenin, who, without the base ingredient of hypocrisy, said he would be for peace and brotherhood until they got guns, and then it would be bullets for their adversaries.

Alan Simpson, the effective and entertainingly quotable former senator from Wyoming, said, "Those who take the high road of humility in Washington, DC, are not bothered by heavy traffic there."

THE EIGHTH HOLE

Grace

"We are never prepared for what we expect."

—JAMES MICHENER

Morality requires intellect. Sure, some actions are kind, helpful, or life giving without thought, but the hard issues require preparation, study, and commitment. Morality doesn't spring full-grown from the forehead of Zeus. Sitting there dumbly in church doesn't make you a moral person.

Leaving aside the theological baggage of original sin, I concur with Christianity's concept that we are all sinners. It is the nature of humankind. We are a flawed species. I don't need to argue this point further; pick up a newspaper from any day, any year.

The Founding Fathers incorporated this view into the architecture of the Constitution. In Federalist 10, Madison writes that we humans are factious—that if there isn't a dispute, we will go looking for one, and if unrestrained, the majority will trample the rights of the minority. The answer is that a single person must represent multiple factions and thus must moderate various views to accommodate as many as possible. Sometimes it works.

What to do with all of these sins? The Christian answer is atonement. "For God so loved the world that he gave his only begotten Son, that whosoever believeth in him should not perish, but have everlasting life" (John 3:16). Only Christ, the son of God and the perfect human, could take upon himself all sins and free humankind, but this view requires that there be a devil and a hell so that sinners who are unrepentant won't get away with it. It is the carrot and the stick. If you believe, you get heaven. If you don't, you roast weenies on your toes aside the river Styx.

What options are there for the well-meaning person who wants to live a good life but doesn't believe in salvation? Here, on center stage, is the word grace—a word with multiple meanings. I don't mean charm or elegance, the little notes that embellish a musical piece, a person of high standing ("thank you, Your Grace"), temporary avoidance of a penalty (grace period), the prayer before a meal, to grace you with my presence, or any of the other past or present uses. Grace here means something like self-forgiveness, and it is both undefinable and multifaceted.

Our swimming teacher, Phil Sanders, made us stand on the edge of the pool with our hands ahead in diving position until we worked up the guts to dive in. Sometimes it seemed as if we stood there for days. We needed a good shove—a metaphysical push. Grace can provide that serene empowerment. Grace can be a way of life. It can comfort and show compassion for others. Grace can be the confidence to acknowledge one's shortcomings and failures. Grace can invite love of self and others and acknowledge that one is loved back. Grace can allow the humility to apologize when one is wrong or has wronged. Grace is a concept—a journey, not a destination.

Aristotle wouldn't buy this for a minute. He thought that love of something that was not eternal, such as another person, was cupidity. Only love of God was eternal. But I am talking here about love of self in a selfless fashion. Grace is a realization that we are a small particle in the universe, and our time here should count for something more than taking up space. That something is service to others.

Another word for what I am talking about is gratefulness. I remember a sandwich maker at Union Seminary who took your order and made your sandwich with such care that I never went through that line without being graced and grateful. During a particularly difficult trial, one of my partners, Bruce Berning, brought a cup of coffee to me at my office at 5:00 a.m. The touch of a loved one on the back of the neck; a sunrise; when the humidity breaks in Washington, DC; a tear down the cheek during a symphony concert. We have much for which to be grateful.

If there is no God (or rather, if that question is unanswerable), to whom should we direct this gratefulness? Does there need to be someone on the other end of the line? I think not. I think the mystery is enough. It is huge and hugely powerful.

The tough part is to acknowledge our human frailty without beating ourselves up to the extent that we are depressed, self-absorbed, or useless. All of us feel like a fraud sometimes, feel lonely, feel anxious. We all fail, disappoint ourselves and others, and suffer. We need self-compassion and self-forgiveness. Some of what we can do is acknowledge our emotions, get them identified, and seek out what is driving them. We can exercise vigorously because sweat is the best way to drive the black dog out of our head. We can recognize that we aren't the only ones in the world or in history who have gone through what we are feeling. We can seek mentors and friends. We can allow ourselves to be vulnerable, and we can avoid obsessing that the worst possible outcome will inevitably occur. A cognitive therapy that works for me—sometimes—is to put the worst case on a stage and mentally draw the curtain.

Ultimately, grace is as undefinable as a sunset. It is what we feel. It is the definition of the spiritual. It is the element that comforts us and gives us hope. It is, in my experience, the closest thing to being in the lap of God.

THE NINTH HOLE

Advice

"Creative minds have always been known to
survive any kind of bad training."

—ANNA FREUD

Most advice is bad advice. This is particularly true of unsolicited advice like "you should get a tattoo, cops don't ever patrol this stretch, one more drink won't hurt, nobody pays that tax." Our heads are for more than holding our hat. We educate ourselves, we learn from experience, we practice what we want to become good at, and yet we take advice from friends or even strangers, and it costs us. Butch Harmon, famous coach of Tiger Woods, Phil Mickelson, and Greg Norman, says, "Taking advice from another player is the surest way to get worse at golf."

We ask for advice when we are unsure how to proceed, but most of the time, we already know, if we take the time to listen to ourselves. Abe Lincoln had the saying that we are all so busy chopping wood that we don't have time to sharpen the ax. Golf like philosophy, or philosophy like golf, is a journey. It is you playing against yourself. What works today may not work tomorrow. Good days and bad days. Mistakes.

Some advice that we give ourselves is destructive like the evil brain worm that says "don't hit it out of bounds" as you stand there on the tee. When I lived in Montana, a state trooper came to talk to our fire district, and he told us that when they have a roadside emergency at night and several emergency vehicles respond, they leave the flashers on only one, because too many flashing lights encourages drivers to get transfixed and drive right into them. Our brains give us plenty of bad advice, so we don't need to go looking for more.

William James wrote that people become what they think about themselves. Winners and losers are self-determined, although only the winners will acknowledge it. Confidence is the sum total of thoughts we have about ourselves, the positive ones minus the negative ones. The more we can develop "bad shot amnesia," the more confident we will be. Jack Nicklaus says he has never missed a putt under ten feet when the tournament depends on it. Whether it is true or not isn't the point. When he is standing over that putt, he thinks he is going to make it. Would you want to be flying with a pilot who didn't think he could stick the landing? Confidence, like courage, is not denying fear; it is confronting it and overcoming it. Practice is critical—preparing the mind and the body.

Blocking out noise is equally critical. If we are distracted by the gallery, the pesky crows, or our own negative thoughts, our results will predictably suck. Likewise, if we consider all of the possible negative consequences of taking a moral stand, like calling out a boss who is a molester, we become moral eunuchs. Sure, we could lose our job, find it harder to get the next job, lose some friends, or have to testify in court, but moral action requires courage and concentration just like the golf shot. The wiggles before hitting, the lining up of the putt and picking a spot to hit for, the looking at the ball with your dominant eye, the listening for the ball to hit the cup—all of these are to clear the mind so it won't mug your body. Morality is a gyro, not a compass. We know what we must do, and the challenge is to not talk ourselves out of doing it. In religion, the liturgy, the repetition, the bread and wine, the smells and bells are to remind us of what we already know.

Here are some examples of advice you may or may not wish to take.

> *"In a lightning storm on the course, I hold up a 1-iron 'cause even God can't hit a 1-iron."*
>
> —LEE TREVINO

> *"Stick your butt out farther."*
>
> —SAM SNEAD,
> to President Eisenhower

> *"Never hit softly."*
>
> —THEODORE ROOSEVELT

> *"You can't go back and change the beginning, but you can start where you are and change the ending."*
>
> —C. S. LEWIS

> *"One monkey don't stop no show."*
>
> —BOBBY RUSH SONG

John Frohnmayer

THE TENTH HOLE

Fighting

"Saying my country, right or wrong, is like saying
my mother, drunk or sober."

—C. K. CHESTERTON

Would I kill another person? That is the ultimate
ethical question, the ultimate existential question.
As a caddie, I listened to the adults, many of
whom were World War II veterans. Nobody had the slightest
doubt that the aggression and immorality of the Axis powers
made killing necessary—noble even.

Dad was appointed to defend a lady named Maxine Click
who was accused of shooting her husband with a single-shot
22 rifle. Twice. While he was asleep. The journeyman district
attorney violated the immutable rule of cross-examination that
you never ask a question to which you don't already know the
answer. He asked one of the Click children, "He didn't hit
you, did he?" The response was, "Sometimes he would kick us."
The jury acquitted, apparently deciding the guy needed killing.

This question came full frontal to me during the Vietnam
War. I had marched in protest. We didn't have any business

there, and the Eisenhower domino theory, embraced by subsequent presidents, that if Vietnam went commie so would the rest of Southeast Asia, was crap. Should I flee to Canada? Was I a conscientious objector? Should I ride it out since I was in theological seminary and had an automatic draft deferral?

As I remember all of those nights awake thinking, or watching the horrifying pictures of our first televised war, of the unanswerable-in-the-abstract questions of whether I would or could kill, there were two fundamental issues: Is someone else's life less important than mine, and what does my country require of me? I decided I could kill. I could defend my family, I would not be gentle if I were attacked, I would protect the defenseless.

The debt to country was harder. This was a stupid war, an unwinnable war, one that we should never have chosen. I didn't for a minute buy President Johnson's justifications, but did I owe my country? I decided I did. I had benefited from life in the United States, and that was enough. Others were being drafted to fight. I wasn't prepared to forsake my country and leave, and insofar as the United States was morally culpable, I, as a citizen, was too. I went, I fought, and I kept thinking, "I am going to be really annoyed if I get killed here."

Even though I was a seminary student, God had almost nothing to do with my decision. I was done with seeking divine intervention in my life. Later, while I was on shipboard, the chaplain said a Christian prayer over the PA system every night at 2200 hours (10:00 p.m.), saying things like, "God knows the world needs folks like us." The sailors would cram dungarees into the speakers. I didn't think god had anything to do with my decision whether to fight or not. This was Caesar's realm, not God's.

Duty to country is what philosopher W. D. Ross calls a prima facie (self-evident) duty arising from the benefits of its safety, education, and prosperity. If my prima facie duty clashed with another moral imperative (for example, a religious injunction against killing), some accommodation would have to be made, and that would be the stock and trade of ethical analysis—an analysis I never made. I decided that if I joined the Navy and went to officer's training, I had less of a chance of getting killed. That's what I did.

THE ELEVENTH HOLE

Friendship

"I wish people who have trouble communicating
would just shut up."

—TOM LEHRER

As a caddie, I assumed that the people (mostly men) who had chosen to play together were friends. Why would they choose to spend over four hours together if they didn't enjoy each other's company? I watched how they acted, reacted, interacted. There was lots of horseplay—hitting another's ball off the green, punching on the shoulder, dirty jokes—they seemed to be having a good time.

They would walk together down the fairway, usually in twos, and talk about stuff. The Medford Black Tornado football team, the weather, cars, movies. Not that "serious" topics such as politics, justice, civic matters didn't arise; but after a comment or two, the topic reverted to the sports page.

Sometimes there would be little conversation for long periods at a time. I didn't find it uncomfortable, because they seemed to be easy with the silence. I don't remember any conversations of disclosure or of comfort: no "my wife is threatening to leave," no "she has cancer; what will I do?" I didn't get the impression that these conversations were forbidden, just that they didn't happen in my earshot.

Such was my initiation to adult friendships. There wasn't much there there. Superficial, vacuous, specific to the moment and activity of golf, and not much more. I know that is an unfair conclusion both because my memory is half a century old and I am judging by what I know now, not what I knew then. That is a valid criticism, but I am going to bull right ahead and draw some conclusions anyway.

Aristotle's *Nicomachean Ethics* (compiled by his son after his death) says that material things won't bring us happiness, although in moderation they are worthwhile: having sex, drinking alcohol, eating good food, and playing golf, he would add, if it had been invented. The real happiness consists of friendships engaged in beneficial activities in which all are working to become the best they can be. This is a spiritual connection with others that transcends the material, gives moral guidance, and does all things in moderation. There is a whole section in the *Ethics* on friendship. The moral lessons, in this state of perfect friendship, become intuitive.

We now know, thanks mostly to neuroscience, that friendships are healthy. They cultivate a psychological sense of well-being, help us avoid sickness, live longer, think more positively. They help us to feel rewarded when friends value what we do, appreciate our humor, share intimate details of their lives with us, trust us. "Yes," you cry, "that is the activation of the nucleus accumbens." I respond, "And it charges up the ventromedial prefrontal cortex." Dream on.

When it comes to the deep friendship areas of sharing emotional information, giving emotional support, and acknowledging interdependency, the men I observed on the golf course scored about zero. It may be that they would have done anything for each other. I didn't see it. While I caddied for women, it was usually in tournaments where the stakes were higher and the singular concentration greater.

THE TWELFTH HOLE

Truth

"There are no eternal facts as there are
no absolute truths."

—Friedrich Nietzsche

T ruth telling was at the core of my moral universe as a
kid. We were punished for lying and given examples
of what happened to people who did, in the law
(from Dad) and in church (from God). Dad told us about
tax cheaters who lied about their income. They went to jail.
He told us about how witnesses in court are sworn to tell the
truth, how juries decide what is the truth. Scripture readings
at church told us that Moses saw God in a cloud as he was
receiving the Ten Commandments, and God proclaimed that
he was merciful, long suffering, and "abundant in goodness
and truth" (Exod. 34:6).

From the New Testament gospel of John, we saw truth
elevated to the center of the Christian faith: "I am the way,
the truth and the life: no man cometh to the Father but by
me" (John 14: 6). "And ye shall know the truth and the truth
shall set you free" (John 8:32). The pivotal piece was Jesus's

trial before Pilate in which Jesus says he came into the world to witness to the truth, and Pilate asks, "What is truth?" Jesus's answer is that those who believe know the truth (John 18:38).

I knew that there was "truth" as it applied to religious claims and beliefs, and there was a different kind of secular truth that was based on facts that could be proved. That distinction—truth coming from religious conviction depends on faith, and truth in the secular realm relies on fact—held true for most of my working-for-pay life. In federal court, a pretrial order would include facts that were agreed and needed no proof as well as the contentions of each party that would require evidence. At the end of the day, if you couldn't prove your contentions with believable evidence, you lost.

In the twenty-first century, facts took a Nietzschean turn. History became what an advocate wanted it to be. Reality and belief merged. Facts were no longer persuasive. Facts were not facts. Truth became what comedian Stephen Colbert labelled as "truthiness": belief that something is true based on intuition or perception without regard to evidence, logic, intellectual examination, or facts.

This state of affairs has cast a cloud over democracy where accurate information is critical to the functioning of the government. The First Amendment exists to protect the press, speech, petitioning of the government, and access for redress of grievances. Those are the tools by which government functions and changes. It is the machinery by which we avoid violent revolution. The press isn't, as some politicians claim, "the enemy"; it is the lifeblood of factual information without which the government by the people cannot function. When we have our own opinion and our own set of "facts," we are in big trouble—and we are in very big trouble.

Philosophers have examined the question of what truth is and how it can be judged, coming up with multiple theories. The one described above where facts are whatever you want them to be might be called the subjectivist view. The corresponding view is that only declarative sentences can be true: a lemon is yellow, George is a man. The true sentence tells us something about how the world is: the sun rises in the east. Saint Thomas Aquinas and John Locke fall into this camp.

Pragmatists such as John Dewey and William James asked about the worth, the value, of any statement or fact. What use is it? What is its cash value? If it works, it is true; if it doesn't, it isn't. Friedrich Hegel, on the other hand, argued that truth will emerge from webs of belief wherein we gather multiple examples to create a coherent universe of beliefs supported by observation and fact. There are probably twenty other approaches, all with advocates and detractors struggling with the difficulty of persuading another human being of anything. The difficulty is mostly in our heads. Our emotions mug our intellect on a regular basis.

Our problem, as a citizenry, is that our sources are siloed. There is a welter of information out there, but we pay attention to little of it and, as a consequence, have wildly different views of what is happening and little common ground on which to respond. We are dysfunctional as a society. Brother Dave, in his days as a university president, compared it to being president of a cemetery: there are lots of people beneath you, but none of them are listening.

A sobering realization that should humble all of us, especially those like myself who are pretty damn sure we are right most of the time, is that widely accepted facts have proved to be wrong. The sun does not revolve around the earth, Newtonian physics gave way to Einstein's theories of relativity, and quantum mechanics will probably be modified or replaced by future knowledge. "Donald Trump could not possibly be elected president," said 100 percent of the pollsters. Philosopher Karl Popper, in discussing the philosophy of science, argued that we can't "prove" anything. Philosophy can only disprove what we currently believe. By this kind of constant testing, we come to the best knowledge we have now with the firm understanding that it is transitory.

Persuadability is a moral feature highly to be prized. It says we are open to learning, that we are willing to consider the new, the different, and the unpopular. Being persuadable is the spirit of liberty.

THE THIRTEENTH HOLE

Intuition

"Don't play what is there. Play what's not there."

—JAZZ TRUMPETER MILES DAVIS

I s there such a thing as moral intuition? Can we sense the right or the good without searching further than our inner self? Do we have some kind of sixth sense that signals the right thing to do without regard to facts, expert knowledge, analysis, or reason? Our current president brags about relying on his "gut," but according to some who have worked closely with him, he is either a moron or an idiot.

Allow me to start over. During my trial lawyer life, I was told of a case where a lady and her family survived a plane crash. It was a benign crash if there is such a thing: the plane went up about three hundred feet, hit a wind shear, came down, skidded along the ground, and broke into three pieces. There was no fire, and the passengers all got out. Afterward, she said her intuition had told her not to go; she said the pilot appeared in their house while they were packing and warned them. Her husband and teenaged son, who were with her on the flight, nodded their heads and said, "That's right."

The distinction may be between explicit memory that we can trace to prior experience or learning and implicit memory: knowledge buried in our heads, the source of which is lost to our conscious memory. The latter is more primal. When we hear a bush rattle, it may trigger a flight response from a time when a tiger lurked there, waiting to eat us. In modern times, what we call intuition can come from overconfidence, where we think we can't be wrong, from ignoring all facts but those that confirm what we already believe or from being totally risk averse on the one hand or foolhardy on the other. Memories can confirm or create intuition by making things fit. Intuitive or hallucinatory thinking can also be a sign of mental defect or disease.

In The Allegory of the Cave, Plato says that humans cannot know the absolute, the perfect, but we can sense it through study and living a good life. That is like intuition. Freud's superego is also intuitive; it is something within us that tells us the right thing to do.

I don't discount intuition, because I have seen it work. Some of the best cross-examiners ignore the rule about not asking questions to which they don't know the answer. They sense that something useful is there even if they don't know what it is. Most of the time they are right. The contrary example of one question too many is given by Abraham Lincoln: "You didn't see him bite off the ear, did you?"

"No, but I saw him spit it out."

Intuition is the stock and trade of the artist. Visual artists talk about recovering from the first paint stroke on the canvas, poets find words coming out on paper as if the poem were writing itself, dancers perform moves they never practiced and didn't know they knew. Painter Edgar Degas put it this way: "Only when he no longer knows what he is doing does the painter do good things."

Feel in golf is similar to intuition. Feel comes from trusting your body to do what it has been trained to do so that the swing happens in a fluid, natural way. The results are much better than if we try to guide a putt or concoct a swing. The source of feel is practice, and to be useful, like intuition, we need to know when and how to trust it.

There are multiple ways of knowing oneself just like there are multiple intelligences. Howard Gardner's seminal book *Frames of Mind: The Theory of Multiple Intelligences* identifies ways in which people can be smart beyond the verbal/linguistic and logical/mathematical that have been appreciated for generations. Musical, visual/spatial, bodily/kinesthetic, inter- and intrapersonal are some of them.

Self-knowledge doesn't automatically spring from any of these intelligences, but knowing that people are differently abled gives a much broader field for appreciating one's accomplishments and skills. The question initially is to discover what one values and then decide if what you are doing with your life is in aid of or contrary to those values. For example, if one values family but spends eighty hours a week at a job away from home, is that consistent and fulfilling? If one values recognition, does it make sense to be a recluse? If one is constantly seeking more money but really wants to go fishing, which is essentially free, is this a considered life, an examined life?

"Know yourself" is a staple of every school commencement address, but it is an elusive and moving target. We are experts at fooling ourselves. The need to examine and clarify our values and then take stock of how we are living our lives—

that is the best commercial I know for studying ethics. Ethics is, after all, the quest for a life of happiness, and chances of finding happiness are greater if we study how to get there rather than hoping good things will happen.

One test that sounds macabre but is nonetheless useful is to write your own obituary. If you don't like what it says, you are not dead yet and can change it.

Humor

"I am a nobody. Nobody's perfect.
Therefore, I am perfect."

—ANONYMOUS

Lots of funny stuff happens on the golf course. A guy named Friendly hit a ball backwards. He topped so badly that it hit the mud about three feet ahead of him, plugged momentarily, and popped back out about three feet behind him. He kept looking down the fairway, clueless as to where it had gone. Al Williams, the pro, was playing a hit and giggle nine with his wife and her sister, neither of whom knew much about the game. On the second hole, one turned to the other and said, "I don't have my ball. We must have left our balls in the last hole." He patiently pointed out that they had hit them—that is what you do in golf.

Humor is hardwired into almost all of us. Babies will laugh at hide and seek, at seeing someone slip and fall, at funny sounds, all without any prompting. As a ten-year-old, I found dozens of things to laugh at on the course. We kidded Eugene McFadden that he was so skinny he could let the wind blow him up to the golf course. Yeah, but how would he land? He said, "I close my shirt." Much of humor is situational and not funny out of context or outside of the group experiencing it. I took a course on humor once, and every representative joke the instructor presented was an absolute dud. The course should have been titled "Where Humor Goes to Die."

Logic is a field of philosophy. So is humor, or at least it should be. Humor is subversive. It can poke fun at the foibles of the rich and powerful in ways that could otherwise prove dangerous or even life threatening to the speaker. Humor can also defuse a situation, return tranquility, and allow us to laugh at ourselves. Humor can be mean. Some claim that humor comes from pain, and the tortured lives of some funny people like Robin Williams seem to support this theory. Among the many annoying character zits of President Trump is that he demonstrates no sense of humor. Would-be tyrant that he is, he could take note of the court jesters in the days of royalty who were there precisely to tell truth to power.

One definition of comedy is tragedy plus time. Aristotle wrote a book about comedy that has been lost and is known only by contemporary reference to it from other materials. Plato thought comedy and in fact all of the arts were a distraction that corrupted society by giving a false description of what was real. You won't see Plato as the patron philosopher of any arts groups.

I don't know if you can learn to be funny. Much of humor is being quick with a quip. Timing is critical in joke telling. A keen sense of the absurd and an eye for human pretension allow for an everlasting harvest of joke material, but few public events are more painful than a speaker whose attempts at humor fail.

People without a sense of humor are difficult to deal with even when they are trying to be nice. At the risk of repeating my instructor's duds and proving that my sense of humor is in the lost and found, here are a few that if not "laugh out loud" funny might draw a smile.

- An elderly man struggled up on a high stool at the ice cream counter and ordered a Sunday. "Crushed nuts?"
"No, bad knees."

- "If truth is so precious, it should be used sparingly" (Mark Twain).

- "Venus de Milo is a good example of what happens to someone who can't stop biting her fingernails" (Will Rogers).

- "Boat 99, come to the dock, your time is up."
"Sir, we only have seventy-five boats."
"Boat 66, do you have a problem?"

- Just you try putting the man who invented the hokey pokey into a coffin.

- The biblical lesson of David and Goliath? Duck.

- What do you get when you cross an atheist and a dyslexic? A person who believes there is no dog.

- If a lawyer and an IRS agent were drowning and you could only save one, would you read the paper or go to lunch?

- You have ten cats? Wow, it only smells like three or four.

- Yo mama is so old she sat behind Jesus in the third grade.

- My grandmother spends all of her time in the garden, because that is where she is buried.

- Her mouth was so delicate and sensual that you would never use the word "piehole" to describe it.

- Four students who spent the weekend before final exams partying were too wasted to make the final, so they told the professor a flat tire had prevented them from taking the exam. Could they take it tomorrow? Yes, but it would be a different exam. The following day, he put them in four separate rooms and gave each an exam booklet. The first question, for five points, was an easy equation they all knew. The second question, for ninety-five points, was: "Which tire?"

- I'm too lazy to exercise discretion.

- "Outside of the killings, Washington, DC, has one of the lowest crime rates in the country" (Marion Barry, Mayor).

- Diogenes with his lantern got tired of looking for an honest man and decided he would look for an honest lawyer instead. His friend, Cleon, asked how it was going. "Pretty well. I still have my lantern."

- No husband has ever been shot while doing the dishes.

- Finally, the obligatory golf joke: "Why don't you play golf with George anymore, honey?"
  "Would you play with someone who wrote down

the wrong score and moved his ball when you weren't looking?"

"Certainly not."

"Neither would George."

THE FIFTEENTH HOLE

Lying

"The great masses of the people…will more easily
fall victim to a big lie than to a small one."

—ADOLF HITLER, *Mein Kampf*

One of the three exceptions to the absolutism of the
First Amendment of our Constitution is deliberate
falsehood. The amendment begins "Congress shall
make *no law*" (respecting religion, speech, press, assembly
or petition). While some jurists have proclaimed that that
means no law of any kind, most acknowledge that physically
dangerous speech such as falsely shouting "Fire!" in a crowded
theater (it is okay to yell if there actually is a fire), obscenity,
and criminal speech such as bribery, forgery, perjury, and
fraud are exceptions. Obscenity is protected under some state
constitutions such as Oregon's and is sufficiently undefinable
that I am not going to try to deal with it here. Supreme Court
Justice William Brennan spent over two decades wrestling
with the concept and finally gave up.

Both our legal and our judicial systems are based upon
truth telling. Every witness in every court proceeding that is a

case or controversy is sworn to tell the truth. Witnesses found intentionally untruthful can be convicted of perjury, a felony. Congressional testimony is often sworn, and intentionally false testimony can lead to contempt, conviction, and jail.

My question is this: Can our democracy survive with two of the three branches based on truth and the third, the executive branch that is charged with putting the laws Congress has passed into effect, unbound by a passing acquaintance with the truth? Prominent newspapers and television channels run daily reports on President Trump's statements. On a single day over a period of 120 minutes, *The New York Times* counted 125 lies or deliberate falsehoods. What are we to make of this? His supporters, including those of religious faith, appear untroubled. In a twisted way, I suppose they could adhere to Jesus's statement in John 8:32 that he, Jesus, is the truth, and the truth sets one free (to believe anything one wants).

Trump is far from the first politician to be accused of lying. Depending on one's political allegiance, all politicians of the opposing party lie to some extent. We are hardwired to want to believe the pieces of information that are consistent with what we already believe. It is called confirmation bias, but there are levels and degrees of truth telling.

In civil law, if I tell you that the puppy I am selling you is a purebred, but I know that I have no papers, and the sire is unknown, you can sue me for fraud and punitive damages. If I make the same representation thinking I do know the parentage and can produce papers but am wrong, you can sue for breach of contract, but you must prove actual damages. Intent is the key, and intentional lying is what I am trying to unwrap.

In her comprehensive book, *Lying*, Sissela Bok says that trust and integrity are precious resources, easily lost, that thrive only when veracity is respected. A pathological liar has no respect for the truth, is unable or unwilling to distinguish it from falsehood, and enjoys telling falsehoods for the pure pleasure of duping the rubes.

The test of a conscientious liar, to coin an oxymoron, is telling lies when facts to the contrary are easily provable. "I was in Chicago yesterday" when I gave a speech in Berlin—as the liar, I am untroubled by the contradiction. I will claim I was joking or mistaken, that I fooled those opponents, ha ha, or will let the outrage slide off my back without comment. Chances are my supporters will love me even more for it. I am being "authentic."

Here is an analogy. At a basketball game last night, I was sitting with friends, rooting for one team, and the guys behind us were vocally rooting for the other. We all were screaming at the refs for what we perceived as bad or missed calls on the team we favored. We were looking at the same game and seeing it entirely differently. So goes our politics.

Kant took the position that lying is never ethically acceptable. One can't look at the consequences, so if captured in war and asked the time and date of the invasion, I can ethically remain silent but cannot tell a lie. I think this is an untenable position. We all lie—"You're lookin' good," "I would love to come to your party but…" "You will be up and back at work in no time," "This student would make a fine employee." We lie to be kind. We lie to keep from hurting others. We lie because it is socially convenient. As a lifelong trial lawyer, I concluded that all witnesses lie in the sense that they put the best face on whatever they say based upon all sorts of personal experiences that make up who they are. Getting to the root of that inherent bias is impossible.

Artists have addressed lying, none more poignantly than Shakespeare writing of lovers lying to each other:

When my love swears that she is made of truth,
I do believe her though I know she lies,…
Therefore I lie with her, and she with me,
And in our faults by lies we flattered be.[4]

Are we in ethical freefall? Is truth still a meaningful word in our bifurcated society? Can we find enough common ground to have a civil conversation with enough agreed-upon facts to serve as a foundation for working together? One small step toward this goal would be a recognition that in most cases it is not a zero-sum game—if I am right, you are wrong.

Take healthcare, for example. Most agree that having quality healthcare available and accessible to all citizens is a worthwhile, just, and desirable goal, but many who have healthcare through their union or their employer are reluctant to change. Others see "socialized medicine" as a threat; some realize that Medicare is socialized medicine and has been around for decades but think expanding it to all would be too expensive. Some either cheer or resist the potential elimination of private insurers. There are probably a dozen more positions. The point is, and this is true of democracy generally, that no one gets a whole loaf. Compromise is the lifeblood of democracy, and if I have so vilified you for holding a position different from mine, if I have made you the enemy, then it is it a win-lose scenario where a solution will prove elusive.

---

4   Sonnet 138, in The Sonnets, Cambridge School Shakespeare, ed. Rex Gibson, Cambridge University Press, 1997, p. 161.

Finally, can there be too much of the truth? Here is a poem from Emily Dickinson:

Tell all the truth but tell it slant—
Success in Circuit lies
Too bright for our infirm Delight
The Truth's superb surprise
As Lightning to the Children eased
With explanation kind
The Truth must dazzle gradually
Or every man be blind [5]

---

5 Poem number 1263 in The Poems of Emily Dickenson, Reading Edition, ed. Ralph W. Franklin, Belknap Press, Cambridge, Mass. 1998.

John Frohnmayer

The Social Contract

"A people that values its privileges above its
principles soon loses both."

—DWIGHT D. EISENHOWER

The idea of a social contract whereby humans agree to live together under a set of rules that will govern their unruly behaviors is attributed to Thomas Hobbes, a seventeenth-century English philosopher. According to Hobbes, humankind has an inherent need for protection when it is in "the state of nature." Here no commerce can take place, no crops grown, no person can be safe from harm, and no buildings, arts, or culture can exist. His famous summary statement is "the life of man (is) solitary, poor, nasty, brutish, and short." The answer is that humans band together, willingly accepting some fundamental rules, in order to have order. Those rules comprise the social contract.

Four basic conditions that apply to all people compel such a contract: basic needs such as food and shelter, scarcity (the necessity to grow crops and produce goods for consumption), a basic equality of human power, and a willingness to work together, which he calls "limited altruism." Through the social contract, people agree not to harm each other and to keep their promises. Laws derive from the agreement of people to be governed, and ethical rules support the laws so that society may function smoothly. People see following the laws and the rules of morality as being to their benefit.

The social contract theory joins utilitarianism, Kant's categorical imperative theory (what you do should be right for all humankind), and virtue theory (there are inherent virtues that should guide us) as ways of explaining the foundations of our morality. As to the social contract, a major criticism is this: "I am not a signatory to such a contract. I didn't seek it out, and it cannot be imposed upon me involuntarily." The social contract also doesn't give guidance on which laws are best and what morals best serve the social order. The rejoinder is: "it's up to the people governed," which brings us back to the criticism, "I did not get a vote. This was imposed on me, and even if it is supposedly for my own good, I should have a right to decide for myself." It is an infinite loop.

Hobbes was surely right about the state of nature. Turn the lights out in a big city like New York, and chaos breaks out within hours. On an international scale, we are in an era of terrorism where stateless groups can attack to destabilize countries and deny their citizens the protection governments are supposed to provide. Nation states have enough weapons of mass destruction to return the few survivors of such a holocaust to the state of nature. It would take only minutes.

There is a widespread belief that the social contract is rigged in favor of a few and against the majority. For example, take the US tax code, all 2,600 pages of it, along with the regulations and case law that if printed out would fill your house. When I was in law school, my tax professor said again and again, "It's a game. It's a game." I knew I didn't want to be a tax lawyer; I only wanted to know enough about tax to pass the bar. But what an indictment of our legal system. You don't have to pay for the government that you enjoy if you are good at the game, if you can afford to hire the best tax lawyers, or better yet, the best lobbyists to write in special provisions that benefit you. That is precisely why the tax code is thousands of pages; it is chock full of special provisions to benefit the least deserving.

Reflect for a moment on political parties. When did the platform of any party play any role in an election? In my experience, never. It was and is all about getting a particular person who has adopted that party's label elected. It is our team against their team, and positions that were reviled by one party will be embraced by that same party in the next election if the standard bearer says so. Politics doesn't do much for the common good when the party out of power has as its sole objective keeping the party in power from accomplishing anything.

Ironically, one of the early proponents of a social contract, the European philosopher Jean-Jacques Rousseau, foresaw the moral swamp of our modern society even while his thought was promoting it. He saw primitive man as virtuous and civilized man as corrupt. Private ownership is at the root of this inequality, he said, and education endorses it. Love of self, which is necessary, morphs into love of having others admire one for one's possessions. Our "look at me" society fits that bill exactly. Rousseau's social contract was to function on the "general will" that would be expressed by a democratic organization of equals. Instead, his thought morphed into the excesses of the French Revolution and the lopsided, republican form of democracy we see today where money trumps everything else.

We need a new social contract, one that we think about, debate, and collectively adopt, that reflects how we want to live together. When terrorists brought down the Twin Towers, crashed into the Pentagon, and hijacked Flight 93 in the attacks of September 11, President George W. Bush urged us to go shopping. I know his intent was to restore a sense of normalcy, but is shopping what defines us? What do we care about? What are we willing to die for? What do we want to leave as our legacy for our children? Do we want to keep living in silos where everyone has his or her own set of facts? Is lying the new norm for public officials?

These are moral issues that have to coalesce into a common societal belief before they can be put into law (for example, a new tax code could not pass until it was clear that it had widespread acceptance.). Laws don't work without voluntary compliance—look at prohibition and the 55 mph speed limit. If most people don't voluntarily comply, a law is unenforceable. That does, in a way, support the social contract theory.

If we are to have a new social contract, it will not be the politicians who write it. It will be the singers, poets, and artists. It will be based on a widespread consensus that what we are doing in politics and national affairs is no way to live. It will start from the ground up, from local communities and groups who relearn how to listen to each other. W. D. Ross wrote *The Right and the Good* in 1930 in which he explained that we have prima facie duties to other members of society including promise keeping, kindness, respect for personal dignity, and the like. In the law, a prima facie case can be overcome by evidence that is more compelling, but if not challenged, it is sufficient. Same with morals.

What appeals to me from Ross's thought is that these duties should be known to all and protected for the good of society. In our age of Twitter, selfies, fifteen minutes of fame, and total self-absorption, egos have metastasized into a social disease. Beyond ourselves is the inherent knowledge that what I should do cannot be separated from what is good for all of society.

How ought I to live? In harmony is a good start: with my neighbors, my fellow citizens, my natural world and all its creatures. In harmony with the metaphysical values of justice, truth, and beauty. If anything in the moral universe is hardwired, it is a fundamental sense of fairness. Let's start there. Beyond that, here are some other suggestions that could help us find a new sense of national community.

1. Democracy is not a spectator sport and the way you get to love your country is to do something for it. Therefore, I propose National Service for a year for every person who is here on his or her eighteenth birthday.

2. Everyone, that is each individual, each corporation, each business entity of any kind shall pay some amount of tax to our government each year. We all benefit from our government, and we should all pay for it. No entity gets by for free.

3. Everyone should have to, be eager to, sing the national anthem. Since when did our national song become a performance piece where we stand dumbly and listen to the latest dipsy doodles of a performer? Doesn't matter if you can sing; get those words out as if you mean it.

4. On a prescribed day every year, everyone should be required to take the citizenship exam. Here are some sample questions: Name one US territory. Who, under the Constitution, can veto a bill? Name one state that borders Mexico. What does freedom of religion mean? Who is Commander in Chief of the military? How many senators are there? What is one thing Benjamin Franklin is famous for? What year was the Constitution written?

5. One day per year should be a national no driving day.

6. Ethics instruction should be mandatory in school curricula.

7. Every five years, all corporations should have to prove that they have paid taxes and otherwise been responsible citizens to continue to do business in the United States. Disqualifying activities would be polluting, unfair labor practices, harmful products, and the like.

8. Campaigns for political office should be limited to ten weeks before the election, and while a candidate could spend unlimited amounts, those expenditures could only be during that ten weeks.

While none of these, if instituted, would fix what ails us, business as usual is not an option if we want to keep our democracy. Just because we can't make it perfect doesn't mean we can't make it better. Artist Eugene Delacroix put it this way: "Artists who seek perfection in everything are those who can attain it in nothing."

THE SEVENTEENTH HOLE

Time

"Dare to think for yourself."

—IMMANUEL KANT

We are all going to die; we just don't know when. This knowledge of mortality separates us from all other species and gives us a peculiar urgency for action. At least that is how Martin Heidegger, an influential twentieth-century philosopher, saw it. An early existentialist, Heidegger focused on our anxiety about the fragility and scope of the human condition and saw our discomfort as evidence that we care. To be human is to be aware that we are in time: in the past, present, and future. The past and present can teach us, and the future, which holds our demise, can compel us to "resolute action." Heidegger joined the Nazi party in 1933, which caused many to disregard his thinking, but his work on the role of time in philosophical thought is useful.

Time makes life precious. How we use time is a strong indicator of what we care about. Time is what history studies, and because time is a resource that cannot be reclaimed, it is the messenger of regret, guilt, and longing. Measuring time in hours, days, and years may be a human construct, but the cycles of the seasons, the tides, the gestation of new birth, and hundreds of other natural phenomena imprint the passage of light and dark on each of us and would continue to do so regardless of whether we had any knowledge of a calendar.

Because of time, ethics requires preparation. We may get only one chance to take action when action is required, and if we haven't thought about who we are and what we stand for that window of opportunity may go whizzing by while we stand bewildered. Happiness here is knowledge—having thought about the alternatives, many of which will surprise us no matter how thorough our preparation, so we can react quickly and appropriately. Rehearsal. It is like a theatre presentation. If you miss your cue, flub your entrance, or haven't learned your lines, you are toast.

The common phrase is that we "spend time." Because the monetary valuation of most everything in our lives is morally bankrupt, we should think of using time, maximizing time by being efficient, being grateful for time, and consuming time with the purpose of making our lives and those of others as fulfilling as we can.

Giving of our time can be one of our greatest gifts. If we give time to friends to listen, enjoy common activities, share joys and sorrows, or be there, we are conferring grace and receiving it at the same time. We can give time to ourselves. Aristotle thought that the greatest good, short of worshipping the gods, was taking time for contemplation—using one's mind to address the issues of life.

Contemplation today is no easy task, since our electronics stick in continually. Can we survive a week without our phones? A day? An hour? It is worth a try. The danger of the electronic swirl we find ourselves in is that our life will run out of time, and we will never have known what it was about.

THE EIGHTEENTH HOLE

Golf's Virtues and the Lack Thereof

"Perfection itself is imperfection."

—Pianist Vladimir Horowitz

Whether one defines ethics as the search for the good, the right, or ego fulfillment, whether one thinks ethics is intuitive, objective, or subjective or derived from nature or psychology, whether it is universal or situational, golf supplies the platform, the stage, the playing field to examine ethical actions and issues. In this chapter, by way of review or summary, or just for something to do, I will catalogue the virtues golf can highlight. As to every virtue listed, the reverse (or the lack thereof) would probably be a vice. A question I will not address is if someone were to list all the virtues in one column and all the vices in another, which would be longer?

- TRUTH. Jack Nicklaus says this is the definition of golf. You shot what you shot. "They don't ask how; they ask how many." It is the virtue of most sports,

John Frohnmayer

perhaps a reason why sports are so popular. At the end of the day, someone has won, and someone has lost. The score doesn't lie. It is unambiguous. It is a number, and if it is the lowest number, it is the winner. It is curious, though, that the winner in golf is the low number whereas in almost all other sports the winner is the one with the higher number. Racing, running, skiing—those are all low-number sports.

- QUIETUDE. This is the virtue of playing within yourself. You let the club do the work, go for the percentage shot, erase negativity from your mind, stay focused and serene.

- RESILIENCE. Face it—life knocks us upside the head. We get up, take stock, forget the bad, concentrate on the good, and start over. Hogan tells us the next shot is the most important, so that is what we tell ourselves.

- SELF-KNOWLEDGE. It is you and the golf course out there—no one else to blame. You have plenty of time to think about your situation while you walk the course. Tell yourself the truth.

- COURAGE. Courage isn't denying fear; it is acknowledging and overcoming it. Granted, hitting a tee shot to a green surrounded by water is not the same as the Normandy landing, but that is a difference of scale, not of kind.

- TRUST. Trust your club, your swing, your putt line, yourself.

- PLANNING. Ethics is all about planning, and so is

golf. Think two shots ahead, know that you will not try crazy shots. Get out of trouble with one swing.

- CONFIDENCE. We can't expect moral certainty— life is too ambiguous. We can develop moral confidence, and like golf, this requires practice.

- FRIENDSHIP. Lots of friendships are situational. Because we do things together, we have a common bond. We have been through the same experiences. We trust each other, are comforted by each other's company.

- CREATIVITY. How dull would golf be if you always played the same course, hit the same drive, the same second shot, the same putts on every hole? That never will happen. Every round is different and calls for our creativity in managing the course to maximize our results.

- PATIENCE. A sprinter doesn't require patience, but in a game that goes on for five hours, a player must conserve resources, maintain concentration, put away frustration.

- ENDURANCE. You will suffer bad shots, bad bounces, bad luck. You will hang in there. That's what you do.

All of these virtues are necessities for the life well lived on or off the golf course. They may not be self-evident in either place. Doing the analysis, asking the questions, and refining the answers day after day is the beginning of wisdom and the stock and trade of ethics.

John Frohnmayer

Now let's consider virtues that don't hang around the golf course. I'm not saying they don't make an occasional visit, only that in my experience, they are hard to find there.

- THOUGHTFULNESS. Totally focused on one's own play, golfers seldom notice or care how the others with them are playing. It is you against the golf course—a singular activity that can block out most everything and everybody else.

- CURIOSITY. You don't care why. Don't give me the reason why the greens are bumpy, the traps wet, the play slow. Irrelevant. Give me the yardage, hand me the club, be quiet while I hit. Don't want to know your life's story, your troubles, what you had for lunch.

- HAPPINESS. There are lots of ways to be happy. Read a book, spend time with a loved one, play with your kids. Golf is not one of them.

- COMPASSION. You don't feel particularly sorry for a partner having a bad day. Get over it. It's just a game. Be a good sport. Those are things we think or say to others that have no calming effect when we are the one hitting the grounders.

- TRANQUILITY. I haven't seen real slug-it-out fights on the links, but I have heard plenty of harsh words directed to self and to others.

- COMMUNICATION. If you are wrapped up in your own game, shooting the breeze with the others is distracting. If you are not paying attention to your game, you are probably playing shitty, and your bad mood makes you poor company.

- GRACE. To be gracious in defeat or victory is a genuine virtue. It can break out most unexpectedly but usually not.

This list is not as long as the virtues golf encourages, but the bad often overshadows the good, so there is no useful equation. However, playing just for fun changes the equation. Forget the score; don't even write it down. Laugh at a bad shot. Enjoy being out there for the pure pleasure of another's company. Look at the grass, trees, and flowers. Smell the blossoms. Bask in the sun or the rain. Watch the clouds. Clear your mind. Does it beat a hike or a walk on the beach? Your choice, but at the very least, golf provides an excuse to get out there.

We live in a competitive society, and there is much to be said for an activity than does not require competition. Golf can be that, although it usually is not. The great thing is that you as the player can decide.

John Frohnmayer

Credo

"The cure for boredom is curiosity.
There is no cure for curiosity."

—Dorothy Parker

A cting ethically is all about preparation. You have thought about the issues. You have thought about who you are. You have determined that you will be a participant rather than just a spectator in life. This preparation has empowered you to gather the facts, to listen critically to arguments, to consider alternatives, and to be persuadable. Thus you can act, not with certainty but with confidence. That is ethics in a nutshell.

Kant dared us to think for ourselves. Kierkegaard warned us not to look to society for guidance, and Nietzsche argued for the will to power without regard to the little people getting trampled. These are wildly different and often contradictory worldviews. No one philosopher's thought will make up our own worldview. Chances are we will pick and choose from many in cobbling together our own playbook for life, and it will change as we change. Nobody said it will be easy; our ethical decisions will lose us friends, jobs, opportunities. The greater cost is to float along not knowing who we are and what we stand for.

Having pontificated over all these pages, it is only fair that I give my credo: this is what I believe.

- I BELIEVE in love, commitment, and passion. This love can be for a spouse, children, parents, and relatives as well as friends, country, nature, and if you choose, God. Love can vanish and requires careful care and feeding; it is never to be taken for granted.

- I BELIEVE in beauty, style, and taste, particularly in music and art. One can do much worse than living a life consciously surrounded by beautiful sounds, objects, and ideas.

- I BELIEVE in compassion, empathy, and service. Life deals people wildly unequal hands, and I have, through no virtue of my own, been dealt a rich and multifaceted one. My duty is to serve others (not exclusively, for I will surely serve myself) and to give of my talents and abilities for the good of society and those in need.

- I BELIEVE in justice, fairness, inclusion, and honesty. The law is called the justice system, but its real goal is finality—solving disputes and protecting society from harm. Fairness, inclusion, and such justice as we can have on earth, collectively, are the work of ethics, and each of us is responsible. Without honesty, we can have neither justice nor morality. Lying denies humanity to the hearer and erases respect for the liar. Promises must be kept. Think of the dollar bill. If the promise that it is worth one hundred cents is false, our whole economic system collapses.

- I BELIEVE in education, learning, wisdom, and reason. It is not an oxymoron to say I believe in reason. Education is the process of developing what scientist Carl Sagan called our baloney detector. By becoming widely read and knowledgeable in multiple fields of learning, we can develop the tools to sort facts and the reason to form our own conclusions. The alternative is to fly by the seat of our pants, guess, believe blindly, and celebrate ignorance.

- I BELIEVE in courage, steadfastness, and efficiency. Courage is the glue that holds all the rest of the moral principles together. Steadfastness is hanging in there to get the job done, and efficiency is getting it done with dispatch.

- I BELIEVE in hard work, dedication, and reliability. If it is worth doing, it is worth doing right, promptly, and well. The ability to rely on others and to be relied on is not just a virtue of friendship; it is a necessary ingredient of a viable society.

- I BELIEVE in mistakes. How else are we going to learn? I believe in grace so that we can forgive ourselves, appreciate all we are given, and be renewed for the next challenge life brings our way.

That's it. Be sure to floss regularly, rotate your tires, and be kind to animals. I'm off to hit some balls; this game has a half nelson on my soul.